The
Cross-Country Skier's
Handbook

The Cross-Country Skier's Handbook

Samuel P. Osborne

in cooperation with the

UNITED STATES SKI ASSOCIATION

Photographs by David Brownell

CHARLES SCRIBNER'S SONS • NEW YORK

To DHK

"You can't start a fire without a spark"
—Bruce Springsteen

Copyright © 1985 Samuel P. Osborne

Library of Congress Cataloging in Publication Data
Osborne, Samuel P.
  The cross-country skier's handbook.
  Bibliography: p.
  Includes index.
  1. Cross-country skiing.   I. United States Ski
Association.   II. Title.
GV855.3.083   1985   796.93   85-14173
ISBN 0-684-18441-9

Published simultaneously in Canada by Collier Macmillan Canada, Inc.—
Copyright under the Berne Convention.

1 3 5 7 9 11 13 15 17 19   F/C   20 18 16 14 12 10 8 6 4 2

Printed in the United States of America.

Acknowledgments

The Cross-Country Skier's Handbook would not have been possible without the support of the cross-country ski community.

I would specifically like to thank Jim Page, the United States Ski Team, Lee Todd, the United States Ski Association, Telemark Lodge, Tom Kelly, Tony Clark, Hank Lange, Bretton Woods Ski Touring Center, Todd Webber, Margo Thorton Webber, the Keene High School ski team, the White Mountain School, Alex Kahan, Jim Stella, Action Sports, Jill Semple, Ted Gardner, Elliot Shapiro, Kathy Hunt, Nancy Hennessey, Karin Robinson, and the National Ski Hall of Fame.

Special thanks are also due the following:

Peter Owens of Atomic Ski Company

Steve Meineke of Salomon/North America

Butch Weiden of Odlo USA

Lasse Hamre of Swix Sports

I would also like to thank my family and Eleanor.

Most of all, I would like to thank Betsey Osborne, without whose careful pen and comments this book would not have been a reality.

Contents

Introduction

Cross-country skiing is the fastest-growing sport in the United States. On any given day during the winter months people all over the country could be out skiing in their backyards, touring on the local golf course, or, in New York, testing the rare snowfall in Central Park. The winter is a wonderful time to be out and about enjoying the crisp air.

Although skiing in the United States has come a long way in the past decade, it has yet to equal the popularity it enjoys in Scandinavia. Instead, in this country the winter for many people is a time to bundle up and head indoors for the four months after Thanksgiving. It means getting up in the dark and going home in the dark. Exercise is confined to working out in a gym with recirculated dry air or caught between cars and snowbanks while jogging along icy roads. The weekends are spent dreaming about the Bahamas. For many of us, snow on the ground marks a time when basketball begins and waistlines grow. Yet there is snowfall in forty-one of the United States during the winter. In Alaska snow stays for well over six months; in Hawaii there is snow all year round at the higher

(UNITED STATES SKI ASSOCIATION)

elevations; in Kentucky, to the delight of school children, snow may blanket the state for a week per year. Snow covers many of the states for two to four months a year. So why not take advantage of the powder and turn a dangerous, icy run into an invigorating ski around the park?

While cross-country skiing is not as easily accessible as it is on the lighted night courses of Norway, Sweden, and Finland, many of us can sample such skiing on the weekends or during the large snowstorms that paralyze our cities. Over 90 percent of the population of the United States live in urban areas that are ill suited for cross-country skiing, but good trails are often within a short drive. While the amount of skiing may be limited, don't neglect the opportunities.

Cross-country skiing, also known as Nordic skiing, can become a welcome addition to your regular recreation. Making such skiing a complement to your current sport is easy and fun. The new rage of triathloning is showing us the wisdom of spreading aerobic training around to avoid injury. Hank Lange, one of the foremost New England triathletes, says, "Cross-country skiing is the perfect complement to my spring, winter, and fall training schedule for triathlons." Cross-country skiing is a full-body sport using all the major muscle groups. It is a "soft" sport without the jarring of running or the nagging injuries associated with racquet sports.

The rewards of cross-country skiing are considerable. A short ski tour on the well-prepared tracks of the local ski touring center, a ten-kilometer sprint in a local citizens' race, or a day-long trek in unbroken and unexplored territory can change your outlook on life and winter. The winter chases most people away from golf courses and public parks, affording you a tranquil place to ski. No loud voices break the stillness; squirrels and bluejays come out of their hiding places to wonder at you as you see them in a new light.

Winter offers views that may be obscured by the leaves of spring, summer, and fall. A ski tour may take you to the pond you swim in during the summer; you'll get a unique view of your cottage or house from the middle of the pond.

The spiritual rewards of cross-country skiing complement the physical rewards. Cross-country skiing at a brisk pace can burn up to a thousand calories an hour. A brisk diagonal stride warms your entire body. Your arms and legs work together to propel you down the track or across the field. A ski tour of two to three hours will put those extra sticky buns at breakfast to good use. A hot rum toddy after you ski is well earned, and it probably won't show on your waist when you're trying on your swimsuit.

It's worth mentioning that cross-country skiing, unlike its sister sport, downhill skiing, is relatively inexpensive. You can buy a good set of boots, bindings, skis, and poles for under a hundred dollars. Some of the best trails are free, or are available for a nominal fee. And you probably have most of the clothing you'll need right in your closet.

A short ski tour can open up your mind to a different view of the world, exercise your body, and give you a new lease on life.

CHAPTER ONE

The History of the Sport

In the world of cross-country skiing, the United States' competitors are relatively new kids on the block. Even so, American victories and technological innovations have made a strong impact on the sport. Ever since the sport came to these shores (whether via Leif Erickson, the Sons of Norway, or "Snowshoe Thompson"—no one is sure) Americans have tampered with and improved the equipment and have established new techniques that challenge this once-Scandinavian-dominated world. Bill Koch won the World Cup in 1982; Marty Hall used Alpine ski wax to make cross-country skis go faster; Tony Wise designed indoor races at the Telemark coliseum.

A CROSS-COUNTRY TIMELINE

The following is a timeline of the history of cross-country skiing, with important moments in the American world of skiing included (see Figure 1.1).

25,000 B.C. The oldest skis in the world were found from this time in the Altai Mountains in Siberia. The earliest ski runners were made from bones of larger animals. Smaller bones were used for skating across the frozen lakes and ponds.

1516 B.C. A Norwegian doodles a picture of his brother skiing on a cave wall; this helped prove to modern man that early man skied. Other archaeological finds indicate that skiing spread from Norway to the rest of Scandinavia.

1000 A.D. Viking sagas portray the Viking kings as superb skiers. Skiing was so much a part of Norwegian folklore that the god and goddess of skiing, Uller and Skada, respectively, are important parts of Viking mythology.

1100 Vikings first use skis in battle. The current Norwegian Birkebeiner race commemorates the ancient battle in which a baby prince was carried to

1.1   *Some early cross-country skiers.* (NEW ENGLAND SKI MUSEUM)

safety from Lillehammer to Rena, Norway. Today's race follows somewhat the same route. During this time the Vikings may have brought skiing to this country. Leif Erickson's brother Karlstenfi could not have gotten through the winters he spent in Newfoundland without his skis.

1521 Gustav Vasa tries to get the farmers of the province of Dalarna to revolt against Danish invaders. He fled from Mora to reach the Norwegian frontier. He was met some fifty-three miles away in Salen, where a group from Mora pleaded he return to fight the Danes. Vasa skied back to lead a successful rebellion that resulted in his becoming King Gustav I. His flight is re-created every year in the Swedish Vasaloppet, an eighty-nine-kilometer race.

1721 Ski troops are organized in the Norwegian army.

1777 While Washington freezes at Valley Forge, the Norwegian army pits troop against troop in open ski competitions (see Figure 1.2).

1843 The first cross-country ski race is held in Norway.

1850 Sondre Nordheim invents bindings that allow control of the skis and produce skis with side camber. Skiers started using two poles instead of one.

1856 John A. "Snowshoe" R. Thompson begins to provide the only winter land communication between western Nevada and California, using his skis to carry mail between Placeville, California, and Carson Valley. Thompson carried over 120 pounds at a time. At two dollars a letter, this was small payment for a rugged ninety-mile trip over the Sierra Nevada. At times "Snowshoe" was skiing on over thirty to fifty feet of snow (see Figure 1.3).

1867 The Alturas Sno-Shoe Club, LaPorte, California, is formed. It is thought to be one of the first ski clubs on the West Coast.

1872 The East Coast quickly follows with the Berlin, New Hampshire's Nansen Ski Club, owner of the famous Berlin jump site.

1888 Norwegian Fridjof Nansen skis seven hundred miles across Greenland. He was awarded the Nobel Peace Prize for this and other expeditions aiding in the cause of peace by bringing together different nationalities to explore the uncharted regions of the world.

1892 The first ski tournament is held in Norway.

1904 The United States Ski Association (USSA) is founded by Carl Tellefsen and others from the Ishpeming Ski Club in Michigan. Tellefsen became the first president of what was to become the governing body for ski sport in this country. The first National Championships were held in Ishpeming at this time.

1907 Asaria Autio of Ely, Minnesota, becomes the first U.S. national cross-country ski champion.

1910 The Fédération Internationale de Ski (FIS), the worldwide governing body for skiing, is founded. The group sets the rules for all ski sport including

1.2 *The first organized ski teaching was undoubtedly military (note the short "pusher" ski and the long "glider").* (NEW ENGLAND SKI MUSEUM)

1.3 *The pole was used to stabilize the early cross-country skier during descents.* (NEW ENGLAND SKI MUSEUM)

1.4 *Martti Lappalainen of Finland finishing in the 17-kilometer race in Oslo.* (NEW ENGLAND SKI MUSEUM)

cross-country, downhill, and jumping. Fred Harris organizes the Dartmouth Outing Club, which still has a national influence on skiing. Every year since its inception this club has placed a student or graduate on the U.S. Olympic team in skiing (see Figure 1.4).

December 11, 1911 Roald Amundsen leads a Norwegian party to the South Pole on skis.

1913 Following the lead of their football compatriots, Dartmouth College challenges McGill University to a cross-country relay race in Shawbridge, Quebec. This marked the first intercollegiate ski event.

1913 Dartmouth College hosts the first formal college ski competition. This carnival, the forerunner of other college carnivals that are the mainstay for college ski competition in the United States, was composed of parties, ski racing, and other winter frivolity. Races of varied lengths were run throughout the carnival season.

1922 The first commemorative Vasaloppet race is run from Salen to Mora, with 119 entries. A resolution at the USSA convention in Chicago recognizes only one class of competitor, effectively closing out the professional ranks in jumping.

1924 The first United States Cross-Country Championships are held in Brattleboro, Vermont. Chamonix, France, is the site of the first Olympic Winter Games.

1932 The Winter Olympics are held in Lake Placid. This is the first time the Winter Games are held on American soil. A Finn, Veli Saarinen, wins the fifty-kilometer contest, where the food breaks at points along the course consisted of pieces of raw meat and soup. After the Olympic festivities were over, Lake Placid ski instructor Erling Strom, Alfre Lindley, Harry Liek, and Grant Pearson become the first people to ski up Mount McKinley.

1938 The National Ski Patrol is organized and recruits twenty-five hundred men for the 10th Mountain Division. Although heavily oriented around Alpine skiing, they become increasingly involved in the sport of cross-country skiing.

1950 The USSA approves plans and authorizes the building of the National Ski Hall of Fame in Ishpeming, Michigan. The building will house the history of skiing in the United States.

1954 The dream of having a home for the history of skiing is realized. The building at Ishpeming is dedicated at the fiftieth anniversary of the USSA.

1962 Bjorn Staub duplicates Fridjof Nansen's feat and skis seven hundred miles across Greenland. Mike Gallagher, current head coach of the U.S. cross-country ski team, wins the first of many National Championships in Brattleboro, Vermont.

1964 Ernest Hemingway writes about the joys of skiing in "There Is Never Any End to Paris" in *A Moveable Feast*.

1967 The United States Ski Association grows to a hundred thousand members, from a membership of forty thousand in 1961. The USSA brings three Swedish women's cross-country ski team members to the United States to help encourage cross-country skiing for women in this country. Clinics are held in all parts of the United States, including Putney, Vermont, where future national champion Martha Rockwell has her first exposure to international competition. Two girls' events—a relay and a four-kilometer event—are included in Junior National Championships in Duluth. The hope is to have a women's team ready in time for the 1968 Olympic Winter Games in Grenoble, France.

1972 Swedish Olympian Lars-Arne Bolling is the Swedish Vasa winner. He wins the eighty-nine-kilometer race in five and a half hours. The last skier crosses the line in thirteen hours. American women make their first appearance in the cross-country event at the Winter Games in Sapporo, Japan. Thirty-five cross-country skiers leave Telemark, Wisconsin, on a cold February morning to be the first starters in a race that would come to be known as the American Birkebeiner. "The Birkie" is now the largest cross-country ski race in the United States.

1974 The Nordic world is shaken. Thomas Magnusson, a powerful Swede, uses Fiberglas skis to win the World Championships in Falun, Sweden. The thirty-kilometer race is run in warm, slushy conditions, which were perfect for the new material. Cross-country skiing enters a new era with the introduction of the Fiberglas ski.

At these same World Championships, Martha Rockwell places tenth in the ten-kilometer race, the best finish by any American woman to date in an international cross-country championship. For her high finish she is awarded the United States Ski Writers' Association's highest award.

1975 In Colorado the first fiberglass skis in the United States are produced by Lovett. The skis revolutionized cross-country skiing in this country. Trak Ski Company begins to produce skis that don't require wax for kick.

1976 Bill Koch of Guilford, Vermont, shocks the Nordic powers as he skis to a second-place finish and a silver medal at the Olympic Winter Games in Innsbruck, Austria. He uses waxless skis to record the fastest leg time during the Olympic relay race.

1979 Allison Owen-Kiesel wins the first official World Cup cross-country race for women at Telemark, Wisconsin. Through the efforts of Tony Wise and others, the Nordic World Cup becomes a reality. Another Tony Wise brainchild, the World Loppet, begins. The World Loppet League is an international marathon race series involving all the major cross-country races in the world, including such diverse races as the Norwegian Birkebeiner, Finnish Hihto, and Austrian Dolomiteenlauf. After much negotiation the American Birkebeiner also joins the fledgling Great American Ski Chase, which includes the best of the marathon races in the United States, such as the Minnesota Finlandia, Presidential Ski Marathon, and California Gold Rush.

1982 Bill Koch finishes first in the Cross-Country World Cup, which is given for season-long supremacy in international cross-country competition.

1983 The FIS Cross-Country Committee, in an effort to control the marathon skate (see page 97), institutes the two-hundred-meter rule, which prohibits skating in the first and last two hundred meters of the race.

1984 The Winter Games in Sarejevo are a disaster for the Americans; sickness and politics hurt their results. Young Swede Gunde Svan skis away with four medals at the Olympics. In addition, he caps a successful season with the capture of the Cross-Country World Cup. Marathon skating is here to stay, with all competitors skating in all parts of the course during World Cup competition. Going waxless has taken over, with the top skiers not waxing their skis with the traditional kick wax in both the World Loppet races and the prestigious Polar Cup races at the end of the season.

A CROSS-COUNTRY HALL OF FAME

Bill Koch

In 1976, wearing his favorite number, seven, this soft-spoken Vermonter stunned the entire Nordic world with his silver-medal performance at the Winter Olympics at Innsbruck, Austria. Using the twisty, windy downhills of the thirty-kilometer Seefeld course there, Koch made up twenty-two seconds on the large Finn Juha Mieto to bring home the silver for the United States. Until this point no American had ever won a medal in an Olympic cross-country ski event, let alone the grueling thirty-kilometer event.

In 1973, after just missing the Nordic Combined (cross-country and jumping) Olympic team, Koch turned his energies solely to cross-country skiing. Cross-country at that point was beginning to feel the effects of technology. Fiberglass skis with fast plastic bottoms were arriving from Europe. Stiffer than their wooden counterparts, the new skis demanded a different style. You had to be physically strong with a large aerobic capacity for the long races.

Bill Koch analyzed his sport to see how he could ski faster. Techniques such as the marathon skate increased the speed of cross-country skiing and threatened to make waxing obsolete. Koch brought back from Europe a technique for converting standard skis into waxless skis.

Bill Koch not only remains a leader on the cross-country course but also continues at the forefront of the advancement of all aspects of the sport.

John Caldwell

Called the "Wizard of Putney" by noted author Casey Sheahan, John Caldwell has been a driving force behind cross-country skiing in this country. A member

1.5 *Bill Koch*
(TELEMARK)

1.6 *John Caldwell*
(NEW ENGLAND SKI MUSEUM)

1.7 *John Bower*
(UNITED STATES SKI TEAM)

1.8 *Ned Gillette* (JAN REYNOLDS)

1.9 *Marty Hall*
(CROSS COUNTRY CANADA)

of the 1952 Olympic cross-country ski team, he is currently a teacher and coach at the Putney School in Putney, Vermont.

As a teacher and coach he has had a hand in the careers of many great cross-country skiers. The list of his athletes reads like the *Who's Who* of competitive cross-country skiing and includes Tim Caldwell, Bill Koch, Bob Gray, Martha Rockwell, and Jennifer Caldwell. In addition to coaching, Caldwell has written widely on the subject of cross-country skiing.

John Bower

John Bower let the cat out of the bag that the Americans were coming to challenge Scandinavian supremacy in the sport. In 1968, John won the prestigious King's trophy at the Homekollen Ski Games in Norway. The King's trophy is awarded to the annual winner in the Nordic Combined. In Norway the American's win shook the foundation of the Nordic ski world, but Bower's victory went virtually unnoticed in this country.

Bower went on to become the head ski coach at Middlebury College. He was the United States ski team Nordic program director when Bill Koch won his silver medal at the 1976 Winter Olympics.

Ned Gillette

Starting out as an Alpine ski racer, Ned Gillette later became a four-event skier (cross-country, jumping, slalom, and downhill) at prep school. At Dartmouth College he decided to specialize and was named to the 1968 Olympic cross-country ski team that competed at Grenoble, France.

After his competitive skiing came to a halt, he turned his considerable energies to expedition skiing. At this writing Gillette will be the only man to have skied on all seven continents. In addition, Gillette has skied around Mount Everest and Mount McKinley. He is currently planning a rowing and skiing expedition to Antarctica. Gillette has used cross-country skis, bindings, and boots for things that people would have never thought possible, including skiing some of the highest mountains in the world. He has endeavored to expand the range of equipment and our horizons with his expeditions.

Marty Hall

"Tough," "outspoken," "critical," and "energetic" are all words used to describe this man, who has done so much to bring cross-country skiing and its athletes kicking and screaming into the twentieth century. A former U.S. ski team coach from 1968 to 1978, Hall took the U.S. cross-country ski team from the backyards of Vermont and brought it to Europe. While broadening U.S. cross-country ski team exposure, Hall developed year-long training programs geared specifically to skiing, and he advocated racing thirty to forty times a year, which flew in the face of conventional wisdom.

Martha Rockwell

When Katherine Switzer ran in the Boston Marathon as "K. Switzer," she set a whole generation of women free to run in open competition to their heart's content. Martha Rockwell has done the same for women who want to ski cross-country.

Virtually unknown outside the sport of cross-country skiing circles, this Putney, Vermont, native learned to ski after seeing a couple of Swedish women compete in her hometown during one of the many visits the Scandinavians would make over the years.

For the next six years Rockwell dominated the cross-country ski scene in the United States. In 1972 she was a member of the first women's cross-country team to represent the United States in Olympic competition. During those years her competition and training partners were men.

The finest result of her career came with a tenth-place finish in the 1974 World Championships in Falun, Sweden. This finish is still the highest placing of any United States women in any World Championship or Olympics.

Currently the coach of the Dartmouth women's ski team, Rockwell continues to influence the cross-country ski scene in this country.

Alison Owen Kiesel

Back in 1967 there were no girls' events in the Nordic Junior Nationals. In 1969, when Alison Owen Kiesel, from Wenatchee, Washington, made the 1969 Boys' Junior National team from the Pacific Northwest Ski Association, she made history and broke down the barrier to the junior development program for women. Kiesel went on to represent the United States in the 1980 Olympics at Lake Placid after finishing second in the prestigious women's ten-kilometer event at the Homekollen Games in Oslo, Norway, in 1979 (still the highest international cross-country placing for any American woman). In addition, Kiesel won the first inaugural World Cup race at Telemark, Wisconsin, in 1979.

1.10   *Martha Rockwell* (ROBERT F. GEORGE)

1.12 *Jan Reynolds*
(NED GILLETTE)

Jan Reynolds

Skiing around Everest, down major peaks in China, paddling along the coast off Baja, or sighting down the barrel of her biathlon rifle, Jan Reynolds is a tough woman to pin down. Reynolds has been skiing ever since she can remember, and like Kiesel and Rockwell has been pushing the limits for women from the moment she put on skis.

Proficient on Alpine, cross-country, or telemark skis, Reynolds was a member of the first U.S. women's World Championship biathlon team. Biathlon requires competitors to ski carrying a rifle two to three kilometers as fast as they are able, then throw themselves in the snow and shoot straight at a target.

Reynolds capped the high-altitude skiing record for women when she skied down the 24,757-foot-high Mount Muztagh Ata in China in 1980. In 1982, Reynolds hiked and skied around Mount Everest on the Circle Everest Expedition with Ned Gillette, Steve McKinney, and others.

1.11 *(left)* *Alison Owen Kiesel*
(TELEMARK)

CHAPTER TWO

Equipment

SKIS

Technological innovations in ski equipment over the past ten years have resulted in specialized skis that are no longer solely wooden. Instead, wood is one of many materials found in touring and racing skis. Different situations in cross-country require different skis.

Cross-country skis can be divided into four types: racing, light touring, backcountry, and telemark skis. Each of these types has a specific use, which should be kept in mind when you are narrowing down your options. Skiing with unsuitable equipment can hinder your enjoyment and can even make the experience frustrating and difficult. Using the wrong skis is like using a mixing spoon that is too small for the job—it takes longer to get anywhere, and you'll work harder (see Figure 2.1).

Racing Skis

Racing skis are designed to be used on a well-prepared ski track. Designed to fit into the grooves of the mechanically set track for maximum mechanical advantage, racing skis are the narrowest available. (The narrowest of these is forty-four to forty-six millimeters—less than an inch and a half—wide.) The edges on the skis are highly pronounced so racers are able to use them to execute parallel turns. While racing skis are narrower than regular touring skis, racing skis are thicker through the waist (the middle of the ski) to make the camber (arch) under the foot more pronounced (see Figure 2.2).

Each ski has a different camber. The degree of camber is especially important in a racing ski; if there is too much camber, the wax can't do its job, because even with your full weight on it, the wax pocket (the middle portion of the ski) doesn't hit the snow. If you place a ski on a flat surface, you can see how the ski curves away from the surface. When you are standing on the skis with your weight evenly distributed, a friend should be able to slide a piece of paper back and forth easily under the wax pocket. Now place all your weight on one ski to simulate the kick of a cross-country ski. If your friend is unable to pull the paper out from under the ski, then the skis are suitably stiff. However, if the paper can be removed easily, the camber may be too great for your body weight; you should consider a "softer" pair of skis. The opposite is also true. If, when your weight is evenly distributed over both skis, a piece of paper can't be slid underneath them, the skis are too soft. Skis that are too soft will be slow in the track and will lose wax more quickly. This test is good only for racing and training skis; for the most part, touring skis do not have or need to be significantly cambered.

Since snow conditions also affect the effectiveness of the skis, many racers carry four or five pairs with them to be prepared for every condition. A softer ski will ski faster in powdery conditions; a stiffer ski is more appropriate for conditions that call for klister. Klister is a cross-country kick wax that comes in a tube and is used for icy and wet snow conditions.

In addition to camber, the biggest difference between racing skis and touring skis is the weight of the ski. Newer materials have reduced dramatically the weight of racing skis and keep getting lighter every year. In the past these weight reductions brought with them questions about the durability and strength of the ski. For a time it was not uncommon when standing next to a racecourse to hear a loud crack as a ski broke in half due to a dip in the track. Now these breaks are far less frequent and probably result most often from con-

2.1   *The range of cross-country skis.*

2.2   *Cross-country racing skis have a high camber and a thick waist.*

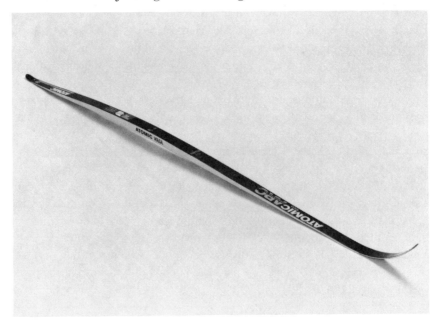

tact with a tree or another ski. Track and material improvements enable skis to stand up to the day-to-day stresses of ski racing and training. Also, the specialization that has resulted in streamlined skis has reduced the exposure to stressful conditions.

Racing skis are reserved for those serious about skiing both in terms of frequency and high performance. If you do not fall into either category, perhaps you should look to a light touring or backcountry ski.

Light Touring Skis

Light touring skis are designed for the person interested in the pleasure of skiing and the benefits ski technology has to offer. Wider than its racing brother, the light touring ski ranges from forty-six to fifty-two millimeters in width. It lacks the pronounced camber of the racing ski and consequently has different waxing needs. In fact, many of these skis are of the waxless variety. The tip of the ski is blunter and wider than the javelin elite tip of the racing ski. The width of the ski allows you to ski both in tracks and during forays off the trail into unpacked snow. The edges are usually rounded, which allows easy turning in light snow; but on hard snow or ice, the turning is much more difficult.

The biggest drawback of the light touring skis is their weight. The Scandinavians have a saying that "a pound on the legs is equal to five pounds on the back." To be used off the track, the skis must be more durable than their racing counterparts, so lightness is sacrificed.

Light touring skis are offered in both waxless and waxable versions. The bottoms of all these skis are made with a material called P-Tex 2000, which is polyethylene-based. These fast bottoms, standard on all downhill skis, are now commonplace on cross-country skis as well. They have made the ski faster and easier to wax as well as easier to clean after a day of skiing.

The light touring ski is the ski of choice for the average weekend skier.

Backcountry Skis

These skis are the grown-up version of the light touring ski. The ski is bigger in every aspect, with both a wider body and a thicker waist in addition to being heavier than its light touring ski counterpart. Built for strictly backcountry use, it is usually too wide (up to sixty millimeters) for use in the mechanically set tracks of most ski touring centers.

Because they are designed for use on long trips into the backcountry, the durability factor of these skis is important. The backcountry is dangerous enough without the added burden of a fragile pair of skis. Like the telemark skis, backcountry skis are used by a small part of the cross-country skiing population. If you will spend most of your time at touring centers and in tracks, leave these skis for those who journey frequently into the backcountry.

Telemark Skis

The telemark ski is often grouped with the backcountry ski. The differences between the two types are becoming more pronounced with the slow but steady growth of telemark skiing. These skis start at sixty millimeters at the waist and are nearly as wide as Alpine skis at the tip and tail. They are cut like Alpine skis and are stiffly cambered under the foot to allow for waxing. The broad width gives stability on steep terrain.

Telemark skiing has made a tremendous resurgence in this country. It was originally invented by Sondheim in Norway during the nineteenth century as a method for touring on large wooden skis. The modern telemark ski is often grouped with the backcountry ski because of similar design. Cross-country skiers are now taking to the slopes on skis specifically designed for the long swooping turns on the downhills. There are now telemark racing circuits. In addition, many alpine ski areas now offer telemark lessons and allow telemarkers on the lifts (be sure to have on your safety straps).

Fitting the Ski

Once you have decided on the ski you want to use, you'll have to determine the correct fit (see Figure 2.3). The ski should be long enough so the tip hits your wrist when the arm is extended above your head. The lengths of skis increase in increments of five centimeters (190, 195, 200, etc.). The chances are that the tip will not hit you right at the wrist. In this case choose on the side of shortness rather than length. As in Alpine skiing, the move is toward shorter skis. The shorter ski is more maneuverable on the mechanically set track, but in the backcountry and on unpacked trails the shorter ski does not provide enough area to hold you on top of the snow.

Wood or Fiberglass?

Is it nobler in the era of technology to hark back to an era of craftsmanship? Or to hold tightly to this our future and, some say, destiny—fiberglass? It is somewhat a misnomer to refer to a fiberglass ski. In many cases it is simply a wood

2.3   *Fitting the ski.*

ski wrapped in fiberglass. But for the sake of argument we will talk about skis made entirely of wood as opposed to those made of everything else. How do they compare?

Wood skis break more than fiberglass skis do. Fiberglass skis delaminate rather than break cleanly.

Wood skis are easier to repair. Fiberglass skis often require major surgery by a person with a doctorate in fiberglass repair.

Fiberglass skis are faster. The P-Tex 2000 base allows the ski to glide like an Alpine ski. Wood skis hold the wax better. A porous wood bottom lets the wax really sink into it.

In the end, it is often an argument of aesthetics versus technology.

If you have chosen a waxless ski, you are faced with a collection of waxless bottoms (see Figure 2.4). If you have the option before you buy, try out a couple of the different types of bottoms. The cross-country ski centers all rent waxless skis. However, each of them offers different brand names, and there are as many types of bottoms as there are brands. Currently, the most popular is the Trak "fishscale bottom," which is a plastic bottom etched with scales that point toward the back of the ski. When you glide on the ski, the scales lie flat; as you kick, the scales dig into the snow. A majority of the waxless bases available today, such as the bear-claw design, work in this fashion. Mohair works in this fashion, too. However, mohair tends to ice up on warm days so has lost favor among the no-wax aficionados.

Remember when you were young and your mother reprimanded you for stroking your pet's fur in the wrong direction? She told you that it hurt Fido because the fur was being pulled the wrong way and when you did this behind her back the fur used to stand up on end. When the waxless ski was first brought on the market, the kick was provided by mohair. Mohair was a lot like Fido hair, smooth in one direction and standing on end when stroked in the other. Using this principle, mohair allowed the ski to glide in one direction (forward) and provided a purchase when the ski slid backward slightly.

Ski manufacturers are always making improvements in the waxless bottoms. One of the latest developments is the milled hairy base. On the bottom of the ski directly under the foot, the ski bottom has been treated so that minute artificial hairs are formed at a forty-five-degree angle to the ski itself. This allows the ski to glide forward more easily than the traditional fishscale bottoms popular in the beginning of the no-wax revolution. These skis range in price from $95.00–$120.00. Currently, Jarvinen, Skilom, and Trak are leading the way with the new technology, but it will not be long before the other manufacturers follow suit with a hairy base of their own.

There are as many bottoms as there are brands, so if you get a chance, test them.

2.4 *Here are a few examples of the variety of ski bottoms available.*

BOOTS AND BINDINGS

Comfort, styling, and durability will determine your choice of cross-country ski boot. Also important is the binding it uses. After all, your boots have to be compatible with your skis. But select your boots first, as it is more difficult to find boots compatible with your feet than boots compatible with bindings.

Boots have gone through a great deal of change. The first ski touring boots on the market were merely miniature and more flexible versions of their sister boots the Alpine or downhill ski boots. As cross-country skiing became more sophisticated, the boots changed radically. While they once looked like hiking boots with a slight extension around the sole, now they resemble running shoes with a tongue or a metal ring on the toe for hooking into the binding.

Pictured in Figure 2.5 are four kinds of boots: Alpine boot, telemark boot, a cross-country touring boot, and a cross-country racing boot.

Originally all-leather, boots are now made from leather, Gore-Tex, plastic, and nylon. How do you choose the right material, much less the right boot? The first step is to find out which boot fits your foot best. Each foot has a different shape. Luckily, most manufacturers make their boots in a variety of materials, so this allows you some flexibility in finding the correct fit. If a size 8 in a particular brand doesn't fit, chances are a competitor's size 8 will. And you'll probably still have a wide selection of materials from which to choose.

Comfort should be the first criterion for choosing a boot. A boot that fits poorly can cut off circulation in your foot, and cold feet make for an unpleasant ski. Always fit a boot with two pairs of socks (see page 40). Don't just pull on two thick rag wool socks or two pairs of cotton tube socks. Wear socks of a thickness comparable to what you'll be wearing on the trails. The boot should fit snugly but not so tightly that the foot feels cramped or tight. Walk around in the boots to see how they fit. Don't be afraid to test their comfort. Then imitate a cross-country diagonal stride (see page 74). If the boot feels the least bit uncomfortable in the store, keep on looking. Imagine how painful the constriction would be after an hour or two of skiing.

Once you've found a boot that is both comfortable and adaptable to the kind of binding you would like to use, decide what material best suits your skiing needs. Cross-country ski racing and race training require different materials than ski touring does. The ski racer's primary concern is lightness. Under almost any conditions light boots will keep the racer warm because he or she moves so quickly. Also, since racetracks are mechanically set, there is little chance that

2.5 *From left to right: An Alpine, racing, touring, and telemarking boot.*

wet boots will become a problem. However, for the off-track or slower skier who might have snow melting on the boots, wetness can be an issue.

Which material is best for your boot needs? Leather, like all natural materials, is breathable and durable. However, it requires maintenance to stay in that condition. After a long day of skiing the boots should be dried out carefully at room temperature. Leather exposed more quickly at a higher temperature (e.g., in front of a fire) will dry out and crack.

In addition, it is important to grease boots regularly so the leather remains supple and waterproof. Leather will stretch, unlike the man-made fibers, which do not to any great extent. Thus a leather boot will conform to fit your foot exactly, which makes the boot much more comfortable.

Preserving the leather on your boots will extend their life and keep them comfortable. After the boots have dried out, use some form of leather preservative on them. There are a number of them on the market that have an animal grease base, such as mink oil. Products such as Sno-seal are good for waterproofing, but they do not preserve the leather. Instead, they coat it with silicone-based protection.

The majority of cross-country ski boots on the market are made of nylon.

Nylon is water-resistant and will shed snow before it has a chance to melt. The boots will absorb water if saturated, but they will dry quickly under almost all kinds of heat. Be careful, though; if the heat is too high, the boot will melt. Nylon boots are not designed for warmth, so if you want warm feet you will have to keep moving around the trail.

Gore-Tex is the coming fashion in boots. Gore-Tex is well known for breathability as well as being waterproof and is the ideal fabric for cross-country ski boots. During the strenuous parts of the ski tour, the material breathes and helps your feet stay dry. Combined with a Thinsulate liner, the boot will keep you warm even when you're standing for long periods of time.

Plastic material is most often found in children's boots. Although it sheds water easily, plastic does not breathe so that sweat is soaked up by the sock, which can chill the foot.

Once you've selected the boot material that best suits your needs, you'll have to choose what kind of boot is best for you. If you plan to stay strictly in tracks for your cross-country skiing, almost any boot will do. I would advise staying away from a stiff boot designed for telemarking (see page 96). If you are going to ski off-trail as well as on established tracks, I would advise a high-top touring boot, which offers good support and warmth, rather than the traditional racing boot, which is little more than a track shoe with a stiff sole. A beginner should seriously consider a high-topped boot, which will offer warmth and support on those cold days.

Selecting a Binding

Bindings, like boots, have changed over the years. Originally bindings were made from woven grass or leather straps, which kept the toe from moving around on the ski too much. The turning capabilities of these early skis were nonexistent. In the days when the speeds in the downhill ski races in the Sierra Nevada reached fifty to sixty miles per hour, that must have been frightening. Grass and leather bindings were replaced by a cable system that partially locked the heel down to the ski and thus permitted the skier to turn more easily. But skiing over hills was difficult because the heel lacked mobility. For the downhill skier this was not much of a problem. The rear binding immobilized the heel and allowed for unprecedented control of the skis and easy turning, especially at high speeds.

The cross-country ski binding, however, had different requirements and took a different course. In cross-country skiing, control on the downhill was sac-

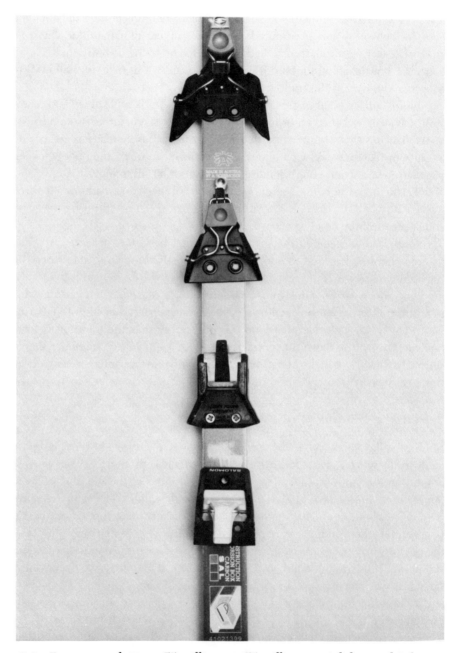

2.6 *From top to bottom: 75-millimeter, 55-millimeter, Adidas, and Salomon bindings.*

rificed for lightness and comfort on the uphill sections of the tour. The binding held the extended sole of the boot with a bail, a piece of metal that fit over the extended sole with a clasp that held the boot tightly to the binding.

The bail or 75-millimeter system was considered the "Nordic norm" and remained unaltered for many years, except that it shrank to 55 millimeters. (The 75 and 55 millimeters referred to the width of the binding itself.) It wasn't until fiberglass skis were already a hit on the market that boot and binding manufacturers began to look at the binding as a place to save weight and retain control of the ski without sacrificing durability (see Figure 2.6).

Cross-country ski races were a good place to test equipment. Racers skied more than anybody else did, and their races of up to fifty kilometers were good tests of durability. The long hours of training gave manufacturers adequate testing time on all new products. Thus it was in the arena of competitive cross-country skiing that the boot and binding innovations began.

The result of this early testing was the grandfather of what is known today as the boot-binding system. Every boot is specifically designed for a certain binding, which allows for better control of the ski because the boot and the binding work better in tandem. Since the boot is locked into the ski, there is little side-to-side movement. Adidas appeared on the scene with the first boot-binding combination at the Olympic Winter Games in Innsbruck in 1976, an innovation that was to be part of a decade of change for cross-country skiing.

Not only was the boot-binding combination lighter, it was also faster. At the same time, innovations in track setting meant that more attention was being paid to grooming ski trails. Both tracks and skis were faster and more durable. But the 75- and 50-millimeter bindings were dragging in these groomed tracks. The new bindings were designed to fit into the confines of these mechanically set tracks, which makes them inadequate for out-of-track skiing. Fortunately, track skiing is more popular and does not require the great support from the boot and binding that backcountry and telemark skiing require.

The boot-binding combination allows for greater speed as well as more control over the ski itself, as the soles are more rigid than the soles of the leather boots that were being used with the 55-millimeter and 75-millimeter bindings. In addition to the new boot-binding system, the innovations in materials have further improved skiing both in and out of the track.

There are a number of boot-binding combinations on the market (see Figure 2.7). While the Adidas system was the forerunner of the boot-binding combinations on the market, the most widely used today is the Salomon Nordic System. In a recent American Birkebeiner, over half of the top one thousand

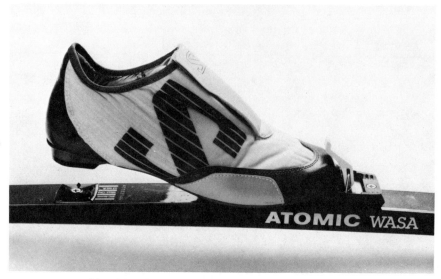

2.7 *A typical boot-binding combination.*

finishers used some form of the Salomon Nordic System. Salomon uses their system with their own boots as well as with the boots of five other manufacturers (Hartjes, Heierling, Jalas, Meindel, and Merrell). Other boot-binding manufacturers besides Adidas and Salomon are Dynafit, the "Contact System" from Trak, Alpina's Control System, and the Artex-Landsem System. There is no "best" combination; find the one that works best for you.

Many of the bindings manufacturers offer step-in bindings that allow you to attach your boot to the binding without leaning over, leaving your hands free to steady yourself. When you have finished your day of ski touring you can use your pole to release your boot from the binding. To incorporate the step-in feature into the binding, manufacturers have had to add more weight to the binding, which, except for convenience, is really the only difference between it and the manual type of binding.

The cost of the boots and bindings will differ among manufacturers. However, the price range for a good pair of boots can be from forty dollars for a good touring boot to one hundred for a top-of-the-line racing boot. The bindings will start at twelve dollars and go to twenty-five dollars for a good racing binding. For the boot and binding combinations you will pay for them separately. Many sporting goods stores will offer you so-called packages of boots, bindings, skis, and poles, with price ranges of about eighty dollars and up. This is more economical, but you won't have as much flexibility in choice.

POLES

Although the three types of cross-country ski poles—racing, backcountry, and touring—are made from four different types of material, the chief differences among the types of poles are in their designs (see Figure 2.8). Racing poles are used for racing or training. Touring poles are used for leisurely tours through the countryside and off the well-packed trails of touring centers. Backcountry poles are especially durable and used for heavy-duty off-track skiing.

Cross-country racing poles have modified baskets that look like half baskets. The basket is designed so that when the pole is at an angle it comes out of the snow easily. The pole is designed for use in mechanically prepared tracks that have a hard poling surface. Off-track, the pole will plunge deep into the snow and do little to propel you forward. The shaft of the pole is stiff and light for maximum transfer of power to the snow with minimal weight. Many of the poles now available on the market have canted pole handles, which provide a mechanical advantage when placing the pole in the snow.

The touring pole has a full basket, which is best used off-track, although it also functions on the track. If you plan to do all your touring off-track you might consider an oversized basket, which will keep your pole above even powdery snow. While touring poles have none of the mechanical modifications of racing poles, they are also not as frail, which is important to the novice skier (see Figure 2.9). At first glance a backcountry pole appears similar to the standard cross-country ski touring pole. However, a close look reveals a larger basket which prevents the pole from plunging deep into the back-country snow. The pole is useful if you'll be spending a majority of your skiing time off the beaten paths, but is not recommended for those who ski mostly in groomed tracks.

When choosing a ski pole it is important to pay attention to the pole's material. Top-notch racing poles are made of carbon fiber. This is the same material used in golf clubs and fishing rods. Sportspeople prefer carbon fiber because it is stiff and light, which means that the power you exert (whether it is the flicking of the wrist to send the fly into the middle of the lake, the golf ball down the fairway, or your body down the track) is transferred more efficiently to the action being done. However, there are drawbacks to carbon poles. If hit against a sharp edge they will break, particularly in extreme cold. Also, the ultraviolet rays of the sun tend to break down the pole gradually. The final drawback is the expense. At close to one hundred dollars a pair, they cost four times more than the average pair of touring poles.

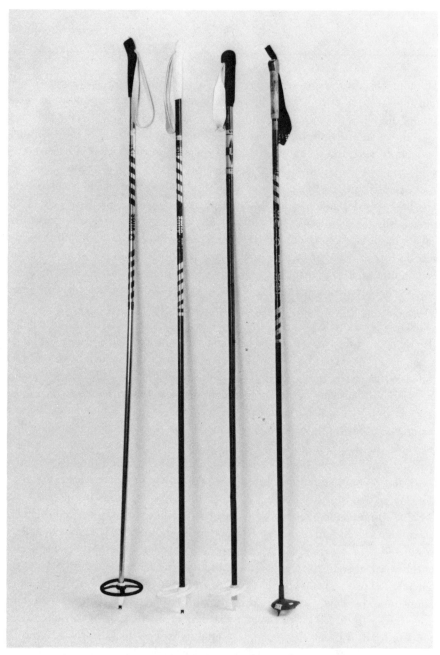

2.8 *From left to right: backcountry, two types of touring, and racing poles.*

2.9　*From left to right: a racing, touring, backcountry, and alpine basket pole.*

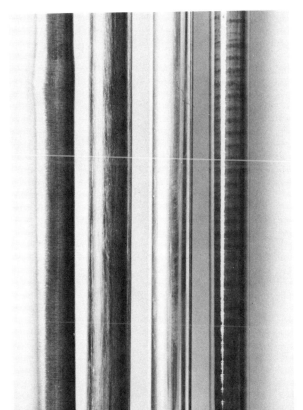

2.10　*From left to right: a carbon fiber, Fiberglass, metal, and bamboo shaft.*

Touring poles usually are made of metal or fiberglass. Fiberglass poles are not as stiff as their metal counterparts, but unlike their metal counterparts, can withstand everyday use. Bamboo poles exist but can be hard to find and tend to be the most frail of all the offerings. However, if you can find them, they're inexpensive, and minor damages to them are easy to repair (see Figure 2.10).

When choosing a pole, remember to take into account whether you'll be racing or touring or doing a little of both. If you are going to ski in mechanically set tracks all the time and are interested in racing in the future, consider buying a racing pole. You'll have metal and fiberglass poles as well as the more expensive carbon fiber to choose from. If you are going to do a combination of track and off-track skiing, consider a good touring pole made to withstand the occasional tree attack or fall. Or if you plan to ski off the beaten path frequently, maybe a large pair of baskets will make the poling easier.

After you have narrowed down the type of pole you want, it is important to buy the correct size. The wrong size pole could result in a strained back or tired arms. If the pole is too short or too long, it will affect your skiing technique and you will lose efficiency. DO NOT use your Alpine ski poles for cross-country skiing, as they are too short to be effective for this.

Fitting a pole is a simple procedure. Stand straight up and put the pole handle under your arm. If the pole fits snugly, it is the correct size (see Figure 2.11).

If you want to get fancy, there is a formula for choosing the correct length. Multiply your height in centimeters by .82. To find your height in centimeters, multiply your height in inches by 2.54. (For example, if you are 6 feet, 3 inches, multiply 75 inches by 2.54; you are 190.5 centimeters tall. Now multiply 190.5 by .82; your pole height is 156 centimeters.) If necessary, as in this case, it's best to round down. Fancy formulas aside, it is important to choose the ski pole that is the most comfortable for you.

The cost of a cross-country ski pole will depend on the type of pole you purchase. A good pair of carbon fiber racing poles can run as high as one hundred dollars. On the other end of the spectrum are the fiberglass touring poles, which can cost as little as twenty dollars a pair. When purchasing a pole it is important to take into account how much you ski and where you plan to ski as well as your current level of proficiency.

Once out on the snow you will want to adjust the pole to your gloved hand. The strap should hold the hand tightly enough so that when the pole is released it can easily be grabbed again, but not so tight that the circulation is cut off, causing the hand to become cold. Remember, the strap is the first place to feel

2.11 *Choosing the correct-size pole.*

2.12 *A proper grip will help you swing and plant your poles.*

the strength of your pole plant, so it won't transmit power efficiently if it's hanging off your wrist loosely (see Figure 2.12).

One question people ask when deciding to take up skiing is whether to rent or buy equipment. If you have never skied before, I suggest you rent for the first couple of times. The day rental for ski equipment varies among cross-country ski centers. A day's rental and a trail ticket should not run you more than twenty dollars. And this is a good chance to test different types of equipment and cross-country ski trails in general. While you're at it, be sure to get a lesson; it will make the entire day more fun.

2.13 *Proper dress will help you make the most of a ski tour. These skiers are enjoying a tour at Sun Valley Nordic Touring Center at the foot of Bald Mountain.* (UNITED STATES SKI ASSOCIATION)

2.14 *Start off your ski tour wearing several different layers.*

CLOTHING

Recent years have seen more and more people moving out of doors, whether to walk on cold fall nights when the nip is in the air or to enjoy winter camping in the cold reaches of Yellowstone National Park while the buffalo huddle nearby. The increased ability to cope with the cold weather during the winter has been made possible by the production of new fabrics for outdoor clothing. Clothing that draws or "wicks" sweat away from your body, and lighter clothes that make bundling up less of a chore have made it possible to stay warm outdoors for long periods of time (see Figure 2.13).

"Fashion" and "function" are the bywords of current outdoor clothing. Words such as "Gore-Tex," "wool," "Thinsulate," "pile," "poplin," and "polypropylene" have worked their way into the vocabularies of even the most inexperienced novices. What do they mean?

Clothes are your tools for dealing with the cold. For a tool to be used effectively it must be used correctly or it isn't worth trying. Using a flathead screwdriver when a Phillips head is called for could strip the screwhead. The wrong clothing will make your time out of doors seem long and uncomfortable. The proper clothing can make winter no more burdensome than a pleasantly cold nose, and rosy cheeks.

The most efficient clothing allows you to move quickly without becoming drenched with sweat. Proper clothing won't become clammy and wet. Pile filling and Thinsulate allow for freedom of movement and provide warmth on even the coldest days. Thinsulate is found in the majority of clothes made for downhill skiing, but it is generally too warm for cross-country skiing.

Here are some simple rules for effective dressing for the out-of-doors:

Layering

My high school coach and former U.S. ski team coach Don Henderson used to tell me, "You can always take it off, but you can't put it on if you don't have it." This simple advice has become my most basic guideline when dressing for outdoors activities.

Always dress in layers so that as you become warm you can take off a layer and place it in your backpack or beltpack (see Figure 2.14). Then, when you stop to rest, you can put a layer back on so you won't become chilled. Your body creates tremendous amounts of heat when you ski no matter what the temperature is outside. You may start out with three or four layers on, but as you move down the trail on a beautiful day in January you could be shedding that heavy sweater. Often racers wear only thin Lycra uniforms.

Layering is an art (see Figures 2.15a, b, and c). Selecting your layers can be a state-of-the-art proposition. First put on a layer of polypropylene, which will wick away moisture from your body and eliminate the clammy feeling often associated with fabrics such as cotton and wool. Next comes a light wool shirt. Wool is a great insulator because even when it is wet it will keep you warm and cozy. On a cold day you may also want a lightweight wool sweater. A light nylon jacket will round out the outfit by cutting off much of the cold caused by wind.

Remember that cotton and denim are not as effective for wicking away moisture as polypropylene. Cotton and denim will keep moisture right next to your body; this can be especially uncomfortable when your sweat meets the cold temperature.

Long Underwear

Long underwear back in Snowshoe Thompson's day was a full-length affair that buttoned up in the front and had a drop seat in the back. The gaudy, often bright red underwear was made of wool and, although scratchy, provided the same warming properties that wool provides today. The one-piece style was for added warmth. The construction of long underwear has changed considerably. The separate shirts and pants are less constricting and more practical. As in Snowshoe's day, the long underwear layer should be the first layer to go on when getting ready to ski.

The best material for long underwear is polypropylene. Nylon threads and the polypropylene are woven together ingeniously to wick sweat away from your body so you'll always stay warm and dry. Wet clothes will no longer be a problem. The materials have to be washed regularly to retain their efficiency. Dried sweat will clog the pores of the poly/nylon blend and ruin its ability to wick away moisture. There are a number of other materials on the market that also make adequate long underwear. The old standby is wool, and while it will keep you

2.15a, b, and c   *These three photographs show one method of progressive layering.*

warm, when it is wet it will become clammy and cold to the touch. Cotton will not wick away moisture and, in fact, will act like a heat suck on your body. Wet cotton will cause your system to work overtime to warm the cold and clammy parts of your body. Silk has a light, airy feeling next to the skin but does not offer the insulating qualities polypropylene does. Pile underclothing is the big brother of polypropylene and is not of any use to the everyday cross-country skier because it keeps the skier too warm. Mount Everest climbers use pile long underwear because of the extreme cold to which they are exposed.

When you go to a store to buy a set of long underwear, the most important thing to remember is what you are going to use it for. If you will be touring for only two or three hours on the trails of the Blueberry Hill Inn in Goshen, Vermont, then your requirements for long underwear are much different than for a month-long expedition with Ned Gillette to the Antarctic. For many of us an inexpensive set of long underwear will do just fine; anything else may be too warm or too wet.

Socks

For many of us our feet are the first extremities to get cold. This usually happens for one of two reasons: The boots are too tight (either because they're the wrong size or because of the number of socks forced into them), or the socks are wet. To prevent this, follow this rule of thumb: The feet should be snug in the boot, but not so snug that the circulation is cut off; you should be able to wiggle your toes freely. Ask yourself, "If I get my feet wet today, will my socks still keep me warm?" Plan ahead.

Materials for socks fall into the same three main categories as long underwear: wool, polypropylene, and everything else. The best sock wicks away the moisture from the foot and helps the foot retain its warmth. The best way to retain warmth and dryness is the layer effect, but don't overdo it. Wear two pairs of socks at the most, any more and you'll cut off the circulation in your foot, which will hasten numbness. Your boot should fit loosely around your two layers of socks.

It's best to wear a polypropylene liner with a thin wool sock over it. The polypropylene will wick away the moisture from your foot. And even if the wool second sock gets wet it will keep you warm.

Knicker socks that go up to the knee should be made of wool, too. Many knicker socks available today are bulky, but manufacturers are moving toward lightweight ones made of a wool and polypropylene combination. These are excellent. However, for the first couple of times you go skiing you should wear a lightweight sock made of polypropylene under your knicker socks to make sure the wool/poly blend is sufficient. You may end up wanting to use just one layer of this sock.

Pants

Before the advent of one-piece racing clothes, there were knickers, and before knickers, birch bark leggings probably served to protect skiers from the cold. The beauty of knickers is the freedom they allow the leg and the warmth they provide the knee. Knees are well-documented trouble spots, and to work correctly, they must be kept warm. The knicker provides an insulating air pocket for the knee during a ski tour and keeps the large muscles of the upper leg warm without restricting movement.

If you are not inclined toward knickers, there are other adequate items on the market. However, let me start the list by telling you what you should not wear: blue jeans. Blue jeans are one of my favorite pieces of apparel off the slopes, but they are not functional for cross-country skiing. They provide marginal insulation, and when wet they suck heat from your body. Constructed for looks, jeans chaff and impair movement except when sidling up to the bar after your tour.

Although wool is the fabric of choice for the lower body, there are a number of other fabrics on the market that perform as well, but just as wool has its scratchiness, they all have their drawbacks. The fabric that has been gaining popularity is Gore-Tex.

Gore-Tex breathes but is also waterproof. The tiny pores in the fabric allow the vapor created by sweating to escape while effectively repelling the larger molecules of water from rain and snow. Consequently this is the perfect fabric for use with polypropylene; the moisture is wicked away from the body and can pass to the other side of a rain- and snow-repellent fabric. However, if you are stopping to rest, Gore-Tex and other fabrics don't provide sufficient warmth. The clothes are designed to move around in, so your body creates warmth.

The same principle is true for nylon and poplin (or sixty-forty, as it is popularly called), materials found in many of the knickers and warm-up pants made for cross-country skiing. Nylon is good for breaking the wind and for trapping warmth but does not breathe, so any moisture that would pass through polypropylene is trapped between the nylon and the polypropylene layers. The moisture then condenses, and the materials become wet. As soon as you stop moving, you will get cold. A combination of cotton and nylon, poplin is windproof but not waterproof. Like nylon it insulates, but instead of trapping the moisture, poplin absorbs it. This moisture isn't trapped next to the body, and when you stop, poplin will provide some measure of protection.

An offshoot of the polypropylene family is pile, otherwise known as polarfleece, or expedition-weight polypropylene. These variations incorporate the weave of polypropylene and nylon and expand it into heavier-weight cloth. The resulting material provides more warmth than the lighter material used in your polypropylene underwear. First used by Norwegian fishermen in the North Sea during commercial fishing expeditions because it did not feel clammy and cold to the touch the way wool did, this heavyweight polypropylene is used in concert with sweaters, vests, gloves, and other items of clothing. Pile lends itself easily to the concept of layering. It is light as well as waterproof. Use on especially frosty days.

A Word About Down

Paul Petzold, founder of the National Outdoor Leadership School, is quoted as saying, "Down is for dudes." It's not very good for cross-country skiing, either. Mittens made of down are usually too warm; the same is true of every form of clothing made from down. I would soften my stance with the old standby, the down vest. It's a great piece of collapsible warmth to carry in your daypack to provide a little bit of warmth insurance.

The trouble with down is that when it gets wet it loses its loft (puffiness) and its ability to keep you warm. Couple this with a tendency to warm you too much as you ski along (with the vest as the exception) and you'll find it's probably best to leave down equipment at home during your ski tours.

Accessories

HATS

On a typical winter day complete with a crisp blue sky, when the temperature hovers at about twenty degrees, there's not a breath of wind in the air, the sun is shining, and the tracks of your local ski touring center have been set perfectly, you can lose up to 50 percent of your body heat through your head. Hats are important because without one, even ideal skiing conditions can be ruined if you are too cold.

Because wool retains its ability to keep you warm even when wet, it is the best material for hats. An all-wool hat will be clammy and wet after a day on the trail, having absorbed your sweat and extensive moisture. Fortunately, the latest skiwear incorporates polypropylene in the headband of wool hats. Polypropylene wicks away the moisture from the area of the hat that comes in direct contact with the skin. The hat should be washed periodically to retain the maximum efficiency of the polypropylene.

Hats come in a variety of weights and types. The perfect hat should be warm but not too warm; it should be snug without scratching. There are two basic weight hats: light and heavy. Lightweight hats are used by racers and good recreational skiers who produce a lot of energy over the course of a workout, race, or tour. Using half the materials of the heavyweight hats, lightweight hats dissipate excess heat and thus reduce the potential amount of sweat and make the hat more comfortable. If the hat itself is too heavy for the amount of heat produced, the moisture will not be wicked away.

2.16a, b, and c *Three types of headwear: a heavy hat, headband, and earmuffs.*

The heavier-weight hats should be used by the casual tourer out for an easier tour and who needs a warm head to maintain comfort. These hats tend to be fancier in design than the lighter-weight hats, although now manufacturers are designing fancier hats for racers as well. The heavier hats will keep you warm, but it is important to remember that once that hat is removed, the potential for getting colder faster is there, because your body has been acclimatized to the higher temperature the hat provided (see Figures 2.16a, b, and c).

Other types of hats on the market, such as acrylic ones, are not as warm as wool nor as effective at wicking away moisture as polypropylene.

If the weather isn't cold enough to warrant a hat, use a headband. It will keep your ears warm and is perfect for year-round skiing, or spring skiing in the East or Midwest. Bring two hats on a tour or when you race. Then, at the end of the day, you can exchange your damp hat for a warm, dry one. You'll be amazed at how much more warmth your body retains.

EARMUFFS

Many of the hats sold today in ski shops do not cover the ears. Also, hats tend to ride up on the head during a long workout. This may not be important during the warmer days of spring but, in early January, keeping ears warm can be a problem. Invented in Norway, lightweight earmuffs are the keys to warmth for many cross-country skiers. Don't confuse them with the bulky earmuffs you see on the Dallas Cheerleaders during the halftime show. The Norwegian lightweight variety are smaller and can be found in many of the cross-country speciality shops. These earmuffs are light, flexible, and made with wool. They are tremendously warm.

GLOVES

When I first started to ski-race cross-country, we used to wear work gloves similar to the ones used by Bill Rodgers on one of his Boston Marathon runs in the seventies. They protected the hand and sold for ninety-nine cents a pair. Then skiers moved into the high-rent district and began using leather handball gloves. These were adequate for shorter races. However, when skiing for two hours at a time during training, the gloves became wet and the hands cold and stiff. A wool liner between the glove and the hand makes all the difference in the world. Even when the hand is wet it stays warm. Now with the liners made of polypropylene, the warmth is even greater. Other liners, made of cotton and silk, are on the market. The cotton does not wick away the sweat, which makes your hands cold, and the silk lacks durability.

Gloves should be leather for durability, but they should be large enough to

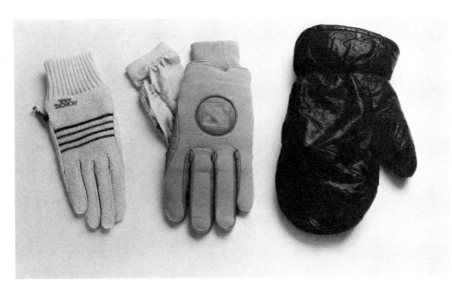

2.17   *A racing glove, touring glove with liner, and mitten.*

leave room for a liner for those cold days when a little extra protection is needed. Again the layering system comes into play. If your hands become too warm during the course of a ski, you can take out the liners and place them in your belt-pack.

What about that old standby, mittens? Mittens are great, but generally they are too warm, it is hard to grip your ski pole, and your hands may become damp easily. Gloves are preferable (see Figure 2.17).

LIGHTWEIGHT VESTS

These have become popular among the racing crowd in the past couple of years. They keep your core body temperature up, which helps keep the rest of your body warm. Racers found them a good alternative to bulky warm-up tops.

SUNGLASSES

In winter the sun's rays and the reflected rays put the ultraviolet ray level at 300 percent above normal, which may cause cataracts. A good pair of sunglasses (preferably polarized) will prevent snow blindness and is a worthwhile investment for skiing during those bright winter days (see Figure 2.18). If you decide to race or if you ski frequently, you might want to buy a Con Shield, a sun visor that can be attached directly to your hat with Velcro. It will shield your face from the sun's rays without fogging up.

2.18   *A good pair of sunglasses will help prevent sunblindness.*

2.19   *These fannypacks are lightweight and convenient.*

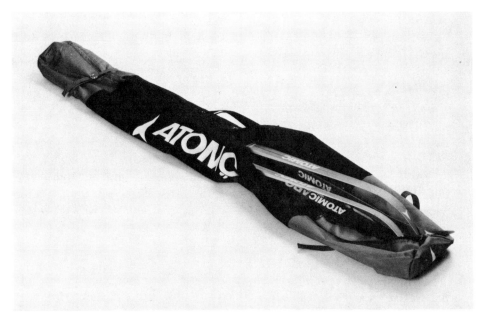

2.20 *Use a ski bag to protect your skis from wear and tear off the trail.*

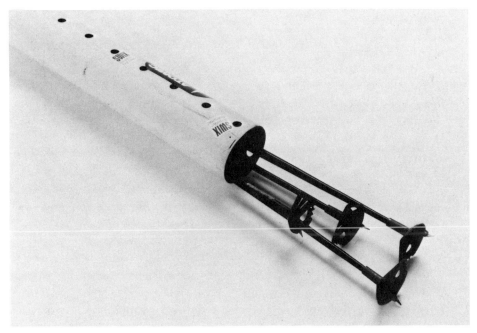

2.21 *A pole tube will protect fragile carbon fiber poles.*

SCARF

A scarf provides a little extra bit of protection. It can be pulled up to protect the face, or it is easily removed if you're too warm.

PACKS

A lightweight backpack or fannypack (see Figure 2.19) will come in handy for carrying wax, snacks, beverages, or extra clothes.

SKI BAG

A ski bag provides excellent protection for your skis on public transportation. Although they're very durable on the trail, your skis may be fragile in the hands of a harassed baggage handler. You can also pad your skis with the rest of your cross-country ski gear (see Figure 2.20).

POLE TUBE

With the advent of new materials such as carbon fiber, cross-country ski poles are stiffer and better able to transfer power directly to the snow. However, they are more susceptible to damage when thrown in with skis and bindings. The pole tube, simply a piece of PVC pipe, will protect those expensive graphite poles (see Figure 2.21).

OVERBOOTS

Overboots do just what they say they do, go over the boot. In this case they add another layer of warmth to the boot on those cold days, or for those whose feet may be especially susceptible to cold. Many of the boot manufacturers produce this item for their particular boots. There are one-size-fits-all models on the market, too (see Figures 2.22a and b).

GAITERS

Gaiters are cloth leggings that extend from the instep to ankle, mid-calf, or knee. They're particularly useful for backcountry touring, as they keep the snow out of your boots and give your lower legs some added warmth.

SKIN PROTECTION

The sun's rays reflecting from the snow can make you particularly susceptible to sunburn, even in the winter months, so take along some Chapstick or other protection for your lips, and a good sunscreen with PABA for your face and other exposed skin.

 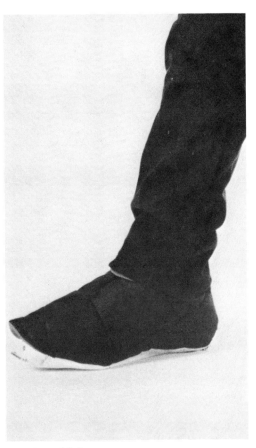

2.21a and b   *Overboots are perfect for especially cold days.*

CHAPTER THREE

Care and Feeding of Your Skis

Man's first steps were a lumbered shifting of weight and a swinging of arms. First one step forward and then another. The left arm swung forward and the right foot advanced, then the right arm followed along with the left foot. Weight shifted back and forth and mankind marched through civilization.

Cross-country skiing is our adaptation to snow. Skis spread our weight out over the soft surface. The skis, with the aid of wax to reduce friction, act like the balls of our feet and allow us to shift our weight and "walk across snow."

Once you bring your skis home from the store, you begin another chapter on cross-country skiing: the care and feeding of those skis. Prepping your skis does not mean you are going to put a Lacoste shirt on them and send them to boarding school. For your skis to perform at their optimal level, it is important to maintain them properly.

Different types of skis require different types of maintenance. A racing ski may require a complete sanding of the bottom with numerous wax jobs to coax speed out of it. A waxless touring ski may require a periodic cleaning of the kick surface along with a couple of glide wax coats at various times during the winter. Proper maintenance enhances the performance of the ski and protects the bottom as well (see Figure 3.1).

3.1 *Preparing your skis well is the first step of a good ski tour.*

PREPARING THE SKI

When you first bring your cross-country skis home, chances are the bottoms will be covered with little P-Tex hairs. (Some skis come from the manufacturer prepared, in which case you won't need to sand them. The no-wax ski usually comes prepared.) Place the ski bottom up on a stable platform. Using a wet or dry 120–170 grit sandpaper wrapped around a sanding block with a surface area of two inches by three inches, begin to sand the ski from tip to tail—i.e., in the direction the ski will glide. After you have worked on the entire length of each ski for ten to fifteen minutes, take a wet rag and wipe each ski down. This removes any particles left by the sandpaper and any P-Tex hairs (see Figures 3.2a, b, and c).

After washing the ski, you are ready to "iron" on your first coat of Alpine wax. You can use a regular iron or the specialized iron available that you heat with a torch. These are very portable. Alpine waxing should always be done on a warm ski in a warm room. The warmth allows the wax to soak into the pores

3.2a, b, and c *Sanding and wiping down your skis.*

of the ski bottom. You can use either paraffin or any of the color-coded glide waxes. The color code refers to the temperature of the snow on the particular day you plan to use the wax. The waxes come with a handy chart to tell you the correct color to use. I would suggest a warmer (the conditions in which these waxes work the best) wax such as a purple glider or a red Alpine wax. The red and the purple have a greater temperature range. These are all available in various ski shops.

Set your iron to a medium temperature. Once it's been warmed up, you are ready to go. Remember, the iron should be warm but not hot. If it's smoking, it means the wax will burn and change composition, which could cause your skis to lose speed. Place the wax on the warm iron with the nose of the iron facing the ski, then let the wax drip off onto the ski. Let enough wax drip onto the ski so there is a thin line of wax running down either side of the groove. Work the iron up one side of the bottom of the ski and down the other. This will leave a trail of wax on either side of the groove (see Figures 3.3a and b).

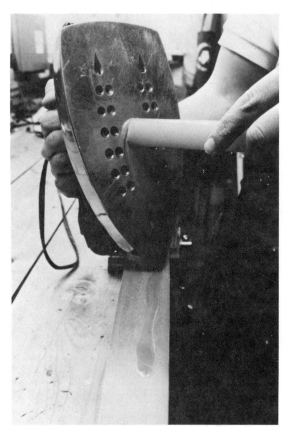

3.3a and b *Heating and ironing on the first layer of wax.*

Caution: Do not put any wax directly under the foot of the ski. In the case of the waxless skis it may render them ineffective, and in the case of waxable, kick wax won't stick as well.

Now take the iron and run it over the layer of wax. Be sure the entire ski receives an even coat. Use an old iron for waxing your skis. I still have a nice coating of silver wax on a pair of chinos from the iron I used for my first wax job.

Let the skis cool down before you scrape them down. Once they're cool, place them back in the stable position in which you waxed them. Place the long edge of a plastic scraper on the bottom of the ski. (You will find ones specially designed for ski bottoms in ski outlets.) Pull the scaper from tip to tail in long,

3.4a and b   *Scrape the ski bottom in long, even strokes, and clean the wax out of the groove.*

even strokes, applying equal pressure over the entire scraper. Uneven pressure will result in a bumpy ski bottom.

Be sure to clean wax out of the groove and off the sides of the ski (see Figures 3.4a and b). Depending on use, this wax job should last about a week. To rewax, simply drip more wax onto the ski, smooth it out, and scrape it off. As you become more proficient at this task you may want to begin to experiment with the different glide waxes available for varying conditions.

Wax and scrape brand-new skis five times. This will give your skis the protection and durability they will need for a long winter of skiing.

WAXING

Now that you have waxed your skis for glide, how do you get kick from them? Kick (grip, stick) is the ability of the ski to grip the snow so that the skier can propel forward. If you have waxless skis the kick is built in (in the form of mohair or fish scales). For waxable skis, wax must be applied to gain the needed kick on the snow.

Two-wax systems (available from Swix, Rex, Rode, and other wax manufacturers), corking, klister, and hard wax are the mantras of the waxing elite. The Eskimos have over one hundred words for snow. All this might drive the most energetic and enthusiastic novice cross-country skier running for his or her no-wax skis. Trust me. With a little practice, you can choose the waxing system best suited to your needs and the snow conditions. It is not that hard.

The simplest waxing system is the two-wax system; you choose between two waxes, depending on whether the snow is wet or dry. Making the choice is as simple as making a snowball. If you can easily make a snowball, and the snow holds together, the snow is wet. To make a great snowball, the snow has to have a high water content. If the snow seems to disintegrate in your hand and won't stay packed into a snowball, the snow is dry.

Most two-wax systems cover these two types of snow. The silver wax works for the dry snow, while the gold wax is the key for wet snow. You apply the two-wax system in the same way you apply any hard wax: Simply crayon the wax onto the ski and cork it smooth.

After you have become confident using these two waxes, the next step is learning to narrow the range according to varying snow and temperature conditions. Adding two more waxes will help you learn how other waxes work. For example, you might add a universal klister (the sticky tube wax used for wet snow) and a special blue hard wax (a crayon-type wax used for colder snow) on top of your first wax layer. Both of these waxes have wide ranges that allow for changes in snow conditions.

Once you have become confident in the use of these waxes, you can handle any of a variety of snow conditions. Similar to technique development, selecting the correct wax takes practice. Hours of enjoyment can be yours when you've made the right choice.

Figure 3.5 is a standard waxing chart. The colors may vary from brand to brand, but each brand will cover all the different temperature ranges. A green, hard wax would be used on those cold, crisp days in January; a special blue when

SWIX HARD WAXES	TEMPERATURE RANGE		SNOW TYPE and CHARACTERISTICS
	°C	°F	
V-05 POLAR	−15° to −30°	5° to −22°	Very Cold (Light Powder)
V-10 GREEN SPECIAL	−11° to −15°	5° to 12°	Extremely Dry (Light Powder)
V-20 GREEN	−7° to −13°	9° to 19°	Very Dry (Powdery: blows easily)
V-22 GREEN EXTRA	−6° to −11°	12° to 21°	Dry (Powdery)
V-28 BLUE SPECIAL	−5° to −9°	16° to 23°	Dry (Powdery)
V-30 BLUE	−3° to −8°	18° to 27°	Dry (Blows with difficulty)
V-35 WORLD CUP BLUE	−1° to −5°	23° to 30°	Dry (For low humidity)
V-40 BLUE EXTRA	0° to −4°	25° to 32°	Borderline Dry (Barely blows)
V-45 VIOLET SPECIAL	0° to −1°	30° to 32°	Borderline Wet (Barely blows)
V-50 VIOLET	0°	32°	Transition (Clumps in gloved hand)
V-52 VIOLET EXTRA (NEW)	0° to +1°	32° to 34°	
V-55 RED SPECIAL	0° to +2°	32° to 36°	Transition (Clumps easily in gloved hand)
V-60 RED	+1° to +3°	34° to 38°	Wet (Snowball easily made)
V-65 RED EXTRA	+2° to +4°	36° to 40°	Wet (Snowball easily made)
V-70 YELLOW			For Moist-Wet Snow, Glazed Tracks
V-82 BASEBINDER (cold) (NEW)	−5° to −18°	0° to 23°	Increase durability on older, abrasive snow conditions.
V-84 BASEBINDER (warm) (NEW)	0° to −5°	23° to 32°	

3.5 *A standard waxing chart.*

it begins to warm up in February; and the klisters when the snow is wet in March.

Once you have selected your wax, apply it to the bottom of the ski in the area called the "kick zone." Depending on the conditions, this area can be from one to three inches on either side of the area directly under the ball of the foot. The two major types of waxes—hard waxes and klisters—are applied differently.

3.6a and b *Applying and corking hard wax.*

3.7a and b *Applying and spreading klister.*

Hard Wax

Hard wax comes in a short tube and looks like a fat crayon. Peel off the outer layer and apply the wax in thin layers in a two-foot strip in front of the heel plate (the plate on the bottom of the ski where the heel of your boot rests). Once you have applied the first coat of wax, "cork" it into the ski using a square piece of cork material for smoothing out the wax. Applying the wax in layers will help it last longer. Now use the cork to buff the wax. After you have corked on two or three layers, test the wax by sliding the ski back and forth across the snow (Figures 3.6a and b). If the ski slips a little, you may want to add a longer kick. To do this, wax a few more inches in the direction of the tip. If the ski continues to slip, a different wax may be in order. Hard waxes are used in colder snow conditions. However, there are a number of warm-weather hard waxes.

Klister

Klister comes in a tube and should be applied warm. Cold klister is difficult to spread evenly. Warmed up, klister can be applied smoothly to the ski bottom. You can use a torch to warm the klister once it is on the ski. Again, the length of the wax application should be about two feet from right under the heel toward the tip (Figures 3.7a and b).

How Does Wax Work?

Snow is in a constant state of flux from one hour to the next, from one day to the next. It is subject to the vagaries of temperature, sunlight, packing, reconditioning, and use. So with all this working and changing of the snow, how does ski wax really work? How, when you apply a certain wax for a certain snow condition, does it help the ski grab the snow and yet allow the ski to glide through the snow so well? The two properties would seem to be in direct conflict with each other.

Each snowflake is shaped with sharp points. Generally, the newer the snow, the sharper the points. When the waxed ski is pressed down onto the snow, these points press into the wax and allow a momentary purchase on these points. The warmer the temperature, the duller the snow crystals become: sharp, round, and dull. So the warmer the temperature, the softer the wax has to be to allow the dull crystal to bite in. On a warm spring day with corn (older, crunchy) snow, the wax has to be soft, so red klister is best. On a cold day with freshly fallen snow, use green, hard wax.

The glide of the ski breaks this contact with friction, which melts the snow. The ski rides on a microscopic layer of water. Thus, for the wax to work effectively, the ski needs a split second to make contact and give the skier a platform to kick from to propel him or her down the track.

Waxing Tips

WAX DOES NOT KICK

If the wax does not kick, try waxing a longer area of the ski toward the tip.

WAX KICKS TOO MUCH

If the snow sticks to the bottom and makes sliding impossible, scrape the wax off and try a colder wax.

NO-WAX SKI CARE

Even waxless skis require care. Fish-scale, mohair, and other waxless skis all attract debris, which sticks into the nooks and crannies of the no-wax ski bottoms. This is especially true in the spring, when klisters are used. The no-wax skis pick up klister left by the waxers, which hinders performance. However, cleaning waxless skis is a simple matter.

Secure the ski in a position where you can work on it. Soak a rag or Fiberlene (a special cleaning material designed for ski wax removal) with ski wax remover and wipe the kicker zone down. Then take a nylon brush to reach the nooks and crannies of the no-wax base. Wipe the bottom until it is free of debris. This procedure should be repeated at least once a month depending on how often you ski, and more often during the spring.

To enhance further the performance of your waxless ski, spray the entire waxless surface with silicon spray before each ski (see Figures 3.8a and b).

REMOVING WAX

Yesterday was a blue klister day, but an overnight snowfall has changed the conditions. Klister will make the skiing in the new powder snow impossible. You must prepare your skis for the new wax. Secure the ski so you can work on it. Take a plastic scraper and remove as much of the excess wax as possible. Now take a rag or Fiberlene soaked in ski wax remover and work on the wax that is left. Once the surface is clean, you can apply the new wax.

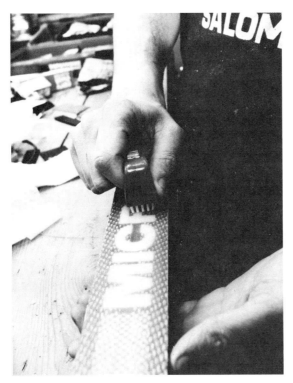

3.8a and b *Use a nylon brush to free your no-wax ski of debris, and spray
the waxless surface with silicon spray before each ski.*

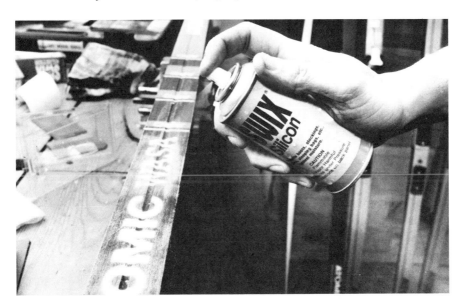

WAX KITS

Following are listings for three levels of wax kits. Choose the kit suitable for the amount you ski and the type of ski you use.

No-Wax Ski Kit (see Figure 3.9)

- ski wax remover
- nylon brush
- small iron
- torch
- glide wax
- scraper
- P-Tex 2000
- rags or Fiberlene
- sandpaper, 200 grit
- sanding block
- silicon spray

Bare Essentials (see Figure 3.10)

- ski wax remover
- small iron
- torch
- glide wax
- scraper
- P-Tex 2000
- rags or Fiberlene
- two-wax system
- universal klister
- extra blue, hard wax
- sandpaper, 200 grit
- sanding block

As you become more proficient at waxing, you will begin to add different types of waxes to those just listed.

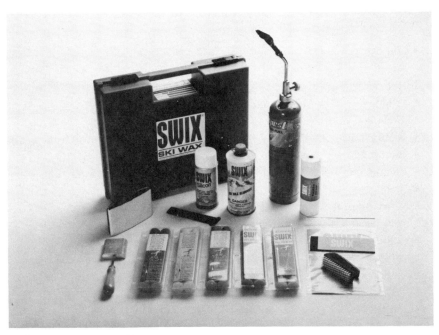

3.9 *A no-wax wax kit.*

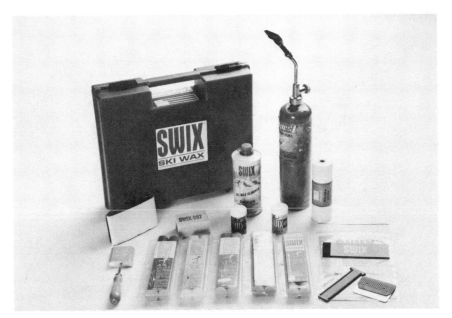

3.10 *The bare essentials.*

Waxer's Wax Kit (see Figure 3.11)

- ski wax remover
- small iron
- torch
- glide wax, four different colors
- scrapers, both metal and plastic
- sandpaper, 120–220 grit
- sanding block
- manufacturer's wax system—both hard wax and klister (one to four sets)
- epoxy
- extra bindings
- extra pole grip
- knife
- Fiberlene
- abrader (a heavy-duty sander for making hairies)
- silicon spray
- binder

All of these can be purchased at a ski shop or through any of the mail order houses specializing in Nordic ski equipment (see Appendix B).

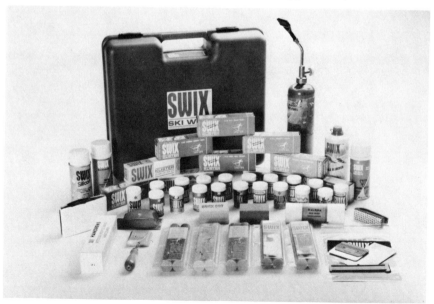

3.11 *The waxer's wax kit.*

UNIVERSAL SOLUTIONS TO TOUGH WAXING PROBLEMS

Binders

Often there are conditions where the snow is abrasive and icy but not enough to warrant using klisters. A hard wax will do, but it is important to toughen the wax and help it withstand the abrasion of the snow. Binders provide a tougher adhesion between the wax and the bottom of the ski. They also help to make the wax more resilient on the sharp snow. Use a binder if you find your wax is working well but isn't staying on for long periods. Aerosol klister binders also exist. Use a torch to warm up the binder and apply it like a hard wax, then smooth it out with a cork.

Hairies

Snow conditions, especially in the thirty-two-degree range, can vary from hour to hour. The snow can't seem to make up its mind whether it would like to be wet or dry, so it glazes. Glazed snow takes a genius to wax for it: Bill Koch and Dan Simenou experimented with a technique, now known as "hairing your skis," at a race in Falun, Sweden, and finished first and second, respectively, while everyone else's skis were icing up.

The technique is simple and may save you from a frustrating ski. Place your skis bottom up, so you can work on them. Take an abrader or eighty-grit sandpaper and sand underneath the kick zone on the ski. Spray the zone with silicon. If the skis slip, try abrading the zone more, or lengthen the kicker. If the ski kicks too much, try more silicon, or apply a light coating of glide wax.

REPAIR

Bottoms

A badly gouged ski bottom, the result of an unseen rock or other obstacle, may make repairs necessary. Secure the ski so it is easy to work on the base. Clean out all excess wax from around the gouge. Clean out the gouge itself with ski wax remover so that it's clean and so P-Tex (available in any ski shop), which will be dripped into it, will adhere.

Once the gouge has been cleaned up, light a P-Tex candle. At first the candle will burn and leave carbon mixed in with the P-Tex. Let this drip off until the candle burns clean. Now drip the P-Tex into the gouge. Give it about thirty seconds to cool, then drip in more. Once the P-Tex has filled up the gouge, douse the flame. Let the P-Tex cool for five to ten minutes. Then, using a metal scraper, remove all excess P-Tex from the ski (see Figures 3.12a and b). Excess P-Tex will slow the ski down.

This would be an appropriate time to apply another coat of glide wax to the ski. That way you'll cover the P-Tex-filled gouge. Be sure to clean the entire ski before you do it.

General Repair

The most common breakage problem in cross-country skis is delamination (see Figures 3.13a, b, and c). Repairing this kind of break is fairly simple. Remove the wax from around the area of the break. Once this has been done, apply epoxy or fiberglass to the areas around the break. Once the bonding compound has been applied, use C-clamps to hold the injured parts in place. After you have applied the fiberglass and tightened the C-clamps down, clean up the excess fiberglass or epoxy resin. Once dried, fiberglass or epoxy drippings are difficult to remove and will certainly hinder the glide of the ski through the snow. If you have any questions about your woodworking abilities, you may want to leave the job to a skilled ski repairperson.

3.12a and b *To repair a gouge in a ski bottom, drip P-Tex into the gouge and remove the excess with a scraper.*

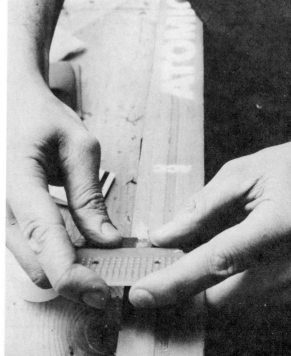

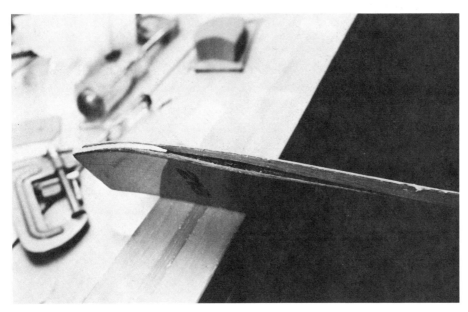

3.13a, b, and c   *To repair delamination, drip epoxy into the break and secure the ski with a C-clamp.*

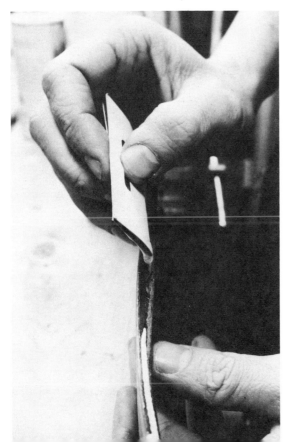

CHAPTER FOUR

Technique

For the average skier, cross-country techniques still are the same as they were fifty years ago. In 1932, Olympians used the diagonal stride as well as the double pole on the flats at Lake Placid. These skiers ran up the hills using a powerful diagonal stride, and in some sections they used the herringbone method. They snowplowed or fell on the steep hills of the Mount Van Hovenberg course.

This next section will review and demonstrate these techniques and introduce some new ones to help you further enjoy a good day of cross-country skiing. But words cannot replace a good lesson from a certified instructor. The following is designed to help you understand basic cross-country ski techniques; a lesson will refine your own technique and give you a chance to ask questions and experiment before you set off on your own. For further reading on technique, please see the Selected Bibliography. Happy trails!

GETTING UP

Free the binding from ice and snow before putting on your skis; it will be easier to fit the boot into the binding. This is especially true of the new boot-binding combinations. Make sure your skis are on a flat spot so they are not as apt to slip away from you. Next, plant your poles securely in the snow so you can use them for support while you are fitting your boot into its binding. This is a precaution so you do not fall and slip right off. Most of the boot-binding combinations do not differentiate between a left and a right ski. However, some of the older bindings do have a left and a right. Some bindings have arrows or diagrams of right and left feet imprinted on them to help you tell the difference. One quick way to know whether you have the ski on the wrong foot is to check if your heel hangs over the edge of the ski. If it does, switch the ski to the other foot.

Once the skis are in place, put your hands through the pole straps (see Figures 4.1a, b, and c). Make sure your hands are relaxed. A common error by beginning skiers is to hold the pole incorrectly, which can quickly tire out the forearm muscles. Also, gripping a pole too tightly can cut off circulation in your hands and make them more susceptible to the cold.

Once you're standing up and relaxed, it is time to ski along the trail. It's often said, "If you can walk, you can ski." Still, your first steps will be tentative. You have to become accustomed to the new attachments on your feet and extensions on your arms. Begin as though you're walking down a city street. When you walk, the opposite leg and arm (right arm, left leg) will lead for the first step and then change over, so the alternate arm and leg lead the drive forward. Now you're "walking on skis." Use your poles to provide a push (rather than merely as outriggers of support) and you'll begin to glide. The use of your arms makes skiing a four-wheel-drive sport as compared to the two-wheel-drive sport of walking or running, in which you use only your legs for power.

Move around in this ski-walk motion and you will begin to get a better feel for the skis and, more important, for the snow. The grab you feel when you push off of your leading ski is called "kick" and is the method for pushing you forward.

While ski-walking, the easiest form of the diagonal stride, your weight should be evenly distributed over both skis. There should be no real commitment to one ski or the other. Try using your poles just to support you rather than give you any real push down the track. Right now, concentrate on learning how your skis work. First, in case you want to head back to the fire, you'll learn the

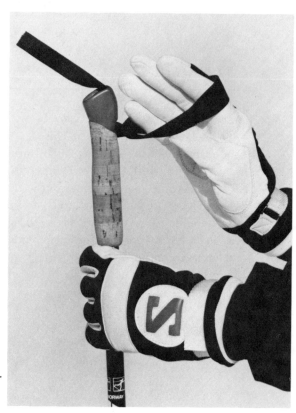

4.1a, b, and c
The correct way to grip your ski pole.

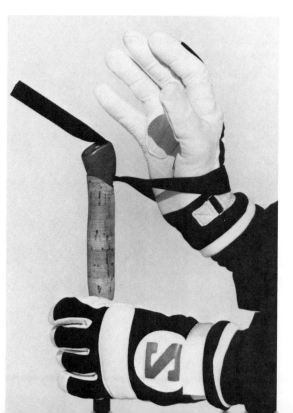

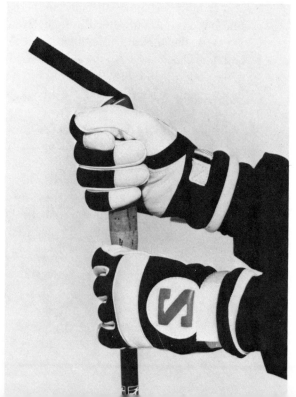

Star Step for turning around. Imagine your skis are tacked down by their tails and you want to head in another direction. Move your skis in tandem to your right or left (depending on where you want to go) at an angle in a simple stepping motion (see Figure 4.2).

A more complicated method to turn yourself around requires you to bring one of your skis around so it points in the opposite direction of the first one. Now you are in a skier's version of the ballet dancer's plié. Now bring the other ski around to parallel the first, and you have turned yourself completely around. This requires a bit of practice, but it is an elegant turn and particularly useful for tight spaces.

4.2   *The Star Step for turning around.*

Once you master this exercise, the next area to work on is your poling motion. This time, concentrate on using your poles once again to move you down the trail. Feel them bite into the snow and then follow all the way through with them in one fluid motion. Used correctly, the poles can save you a lot of wasted energy when skiing down the trail.

Figures 4.3a and b detail the easy diagonal, the beginner's basic steps. The weight is spread evenly over both skis. The poles are placed evenly into the snow rather than thrust there with power and are used for balance.

Once the easy diagonal has been mastered and you begin to feel comfortable on skis, you may move on, to the medium diagonal. With this step your weight shifts from ski to ski and results in the beginning of knee drive, a more forceful kick, a longer glide, and smoother poling. Unlike the easy diagonal, in which your weight is split evenly between both skis, now when you glide onto the leading ski you're committing your weight to it.

Stop a minute and flex your knee forward. See how the ankle flexes with it. When you begin to ski, this action absorbs bumps and allows you to move forward on the ski itself. Now flex the knee forward and check the sole of your foot to find where your body weight is. If you feel weight on the ball of your foot, your weight is forward, where it should be. If you feel pressure on your heel, your weight could be too far back. Get the weight forward and train yourself to ski with it forward. This may not come naturally at first.

The upper body should be positioned in a forward angle, too, well over the gliding ski. The farther forward you are, the easier it is to bring the back ski

4.3a and b *The easy diagonal.*

forward to begin the next drive. It is easier to kick because the ski is compressed into the snow. You can put more power into your poling action as well. The medium diagonal is also known as the touring diagonal.

Figures 4.4a and b detail the differences between an easy and a medium diagonal. In the medium diagonal, the trailing ski is raised off the snow, signifying some weight transfer to the gliding ski. The body position and therefore the weight are mostly over the gliding ski. The body tilts forward instead of straight up and down. The knee and ankle angles are contributing to this forward angle. The pole is thrust into the snow rather than placed on the surface and produces power for forward motion.

The last movement in the diagonal series is the fast or racing diagonal. It requires a strong upper body and an ability to commit to the gliding ski from the kicking ski in a split second. A full-extension diagonal is marked by a full glide on one ski, with the trailing ski raised in the back and poised to drive forward in the kick, and with the poles bent from the power transferred to them during the drive phase.

A racer in full stride shows the maximum power of the fast diagonal at its best. In comparison to the medium diagonal, each facet is extended. The trailing ski is at maximum height and ready to drive forward. The body position is fully foward and over the gliding ski, with a complete commitment to that position. (The ski must be gliding forward, or the skier will end up on his or her nose.) The pole is driven in with force. Another fast diagonal stride will follow.

4.4a and b *The medium diagonal.*

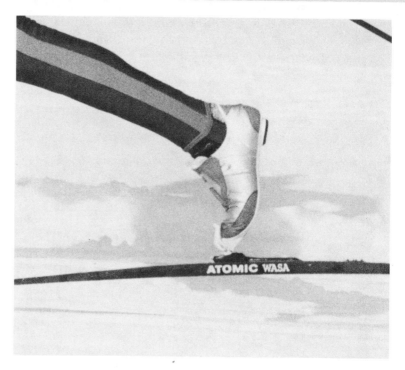

4.5a, b, c, d, and e   *The fast diagonal. The close-up demonstrates the full extension of the foot.*

DOUBLE POLE

Often while you ski you may be going too quickly to use the diagonal stride, or too slowly to use a tuck or other downhill techniques. The technique to use then in the double pole. This simply means using the two poles to drive yourself forward with no help from your legs.

As you can see from Figures 4.6a, b, and c, as the poles are driven into the snow together, the arms are slightly bent to initiate the thrust, and the stomach contracts to bring more power to the thrust. The upper body bends at a ninety-degree angle to the lower body (any more than a ninety-degree angle and power is lost). Then the upper body is raised up and the hands are brought forward for another poling motion. The motion should be smooth.

4.6a, b, and c   *The double pole.*

4.7a, b, and c   *The double pole with kick.*

DOUBLE POLE WITH KICK

A variation on the double pole is the double pole with kick. As you raise your arms, you also kick. Your back then transfers the extra energy to a double pole action. Some skiers feel that the extra kick gives them more leverage than a straight double pole. This technique is used when double poling is too slow and the diagonal is too fast.

The kick is initiated as the hands come up, and the trailing ski is driven forward during the thrust phase of the poles (see Figures 4.7a, b, and c). You should feel comfortable on skis before you try this somewhat difficult balancing act.

COMMON ERRORS

Using the Poles for Balance

Your poles can provide a great deal of the power to send you down the track. However, use of the poles to hold you up rather than propel you forward will only negate the positive effects of the thrust (see Figure 4.8).

Lack of Commitment to the Gliding Ski

Getting your body over the gliding ski means committing to the ski itself. This marks the transition from the easy diagonal to true cross-country skiing (see Figure 4.9).

Jerky Poling Motion

The pole should drive through on the same plane in a smooth motion. To move out of this plane is a waste of energy (see Figure 4.10).

Unsteady Upper Body

The upper body should remain fairly stable during the entire diagonal stride. Think of it as an engine being transported down the track by the legs and arms.

Inflexible Ankle and Knee Joints

Stretching out before you ski can help you relax. Tension in your joints while skiing can cause cramps, tire you out, and promote injury.

4.8   *Using the poles for balance will negate the effect of your thrust.*

4.9 *This skier's lack of commitment to the gliding ski inhibits the smooth diagonal.*

4.10 *This skier is wasting energy by using a jerky poling motion.*

UPHILLS

Uphills can be short, long, wide, thin, gradual, or steep. Each can be tackled with a different technique, or your approach can be varied. Say you have near your house a short, steep hill on which you practice. If you're getting back into shape, you may choose to sidestep up the hill because you're not strong enough to use other methods. Later in the winter, as you get in better shape, you can use the herringbone. Then, in a training session for a race, you can mount the hill using a running technique. Finally, the snow the day of the race may be hard and fast, and you'll be able to ski a slightly more strenuous diagonal over it. Four techniques for the same hill, but different conditions and physical shape.

There are four major techniques for skiing uphill: skiing in a modified diagonal stride; running up (which uses more upper body strength and a faster foot motion); the herringbone; and the easiest, sidestepping. Proficient skiers use different techniques according to the conditions, while beginners can rely on the easier sidestep and herringbone for most uphills.

Sidestepping

Sidestepping is the easiest technique to master. It is time-consuming, but it requires less energy than the other three methods. Place your skis perpendicular to the slope of the hill and begin to step up sideways. As you step up the hill, remember to keep your knees angled in toward the slope. This causes the edges of your skis to dig into the side of the hill and provide a stable platform. Place your poles on either side to provide balance and a slight lift each time you move onto the next step (see Figures 4.11a and b).

Herringbone

Remember back when you were learning the "Star Step"? When you used the method for changing direction in which the tips of your skis were spread out with the heels together so your skis formed a "V," you were doing a herringbone on the flats. Now let's take this position to a slight hill. Notice as you spread the tips of your skis father apart, keeping the tails close together, how the bottoms of the skis angle into the snow and your knees drop down. Place your poles in the snow outside the skis and you're in the perfect position to herringbone. Now walk up the hill.

Unlike the diagonal, in which your opposite arm and leg move together, to herringbone you move the arm and leg of the same side together. Once a stable platform is set, the opposite side moves up to form the other line of the "V." The degree of each movement depends on steepness, track preparation, and physical conditioning.

The herringbone technique allows you to rest in the middle of hills and can provide momentary stability if you slip while skiing or running uphill.

In Figure 4.12 note how the skis are positioned. The steeper the hill, the wider the "V" needs to be, so you do not slip backward. The knees are bent inward so the edges of the ski cut into the snow. The angle provides a steady platform for the ski. The body is slightly forward, and the poles are angled into the snow to provide a significant amount of thrust. Note how the arm and leg come through together.

4.11a and b *Sidestepping uphill. Note how the skier keeps her knees angled into the slope so the edges of her skis dig in and provide a stable platform.*

4.12   *The herringbone.*

Uphill Diagonal

The uphill diagonal technique is an exaggeration of the diagonal technique you learned for the flats. The body must be kept perpendicular to the snow. Leaning too far forward will cause the skis to shoot out the back. Leaning too far back is inefficient: You waste energy pulling yourself up the hill. The majority of weight must be kept on the ball of the kicking foot. To do this, remember to lead with the kicking foot. The poles should be thrust with emphasis into the snow; this will provide the lift necessary to get you up the hill.

As you move up the hill, it is important to transfer body weight from ski to ski in a rolling motion, with the weight going from back to front as you move onto the gliding ski for the gliding phase. The speed with and extent to which this happens depends on the steepness of the hill. You may have to experiment. In this particular uphill technique there is still glide, but it is not as pronounced as the glide in the flat diagonal. This is the most energy-efficient way to get up a hill.

Figures 4.13a, b, and c show a skier skiing up a hill, using a slightly different body position than the skier on the flat. Note the importance of a loose hinging of the knee and ankle.

4.13a, b, and c   *The uphill diagonal.*

4.14a, b, and c   *The uphill run.*

Running

When the glide has gone out of an uphill diagonal, shorten your stride and pick up the rate. You can "run" up the hill. This technique requires a great deal of energy, as all the limbs are moving at a higher rate of speed than in the uphill diagonal. The skier does little gliding but more running. He or she lands on the skis and climbs the hill with more help from the arms. It is important when "running" to wax your skis correctly, as slipping may tire the arms out.

As you can see from Figures 4.14a, b, and c, the running skier leans forward on his toes. Without poles it might appear as if he were foot-running up the hill. Before he falls on his nose, his foot comes forward to save him and gives him another platform off which to run. Again, this technique requires a great deal of energy, but it can help keep your momentum going on short hills.

4.15 *This skier's weight is too far forward.*

COMMON MISTAKES WHILE SKIING UPHILL

Weight Too Far Forward

If your weight is too far forward, the skis will slip out from underneath you (see Figure 4.15).

Weight Too Far Back

If your weight is too far back, your wax won't grab hold. When your weight is on the ski, it will slip out from underneath you (see Figure 4.16).

Too Much Weight on the Pole

While running on skis, don't place too much emphasis on the poles for power because this tires the arms out and does not give the wax a chance to do its job (see Figure 4.17).

4.16   *This skier's weight is too far backward.*

"V" Not Wide Enough

If the tips of your skis are not spread far enough apart, they will slide backward. The same will happen if the tails are not close enough together. As the tips are spread, the tails should almost touch (see Figure 4.18).

Tails Too Close Together

As you move up the hill using the herringbone, you don't want the tails so close together that they cross each other and impede movement.

DOWNHILL SKIING

There are several ways of skiing downhill. Different techniques will be appropriate according to your physical condition, your proficiency as a skier, snow conditions, and the steepness of the hill.

At most of the touring centers you will visit this winter, the trails will be marked so you will know the difficulty of both downhills and uphills before you begin. For the most part the trails will also be groomed, but it's important to master a number of downhill techniques for use when you need them.

There are always questions to ask yourself before you choose a method. Am I too tired to attempt a full snowplow down this long section of trail? Is it too steep to ski straight down? Is the snow so sloppy that I run the risk of catching an edge? Will I need to make a sharp turn to avoid that tree?

Skate turns, parallel turns and stops, snowplow, half snowplow, and sideslip are all downhill techniques. A hill that has been well groomed one day may be easily negotiated using the snowplow technique. Icy conditions the next day may warrant the use of the sideslip. Again, each section has to be evaluated on its own each day.

Sideslip

In the beginning, downhill sections may seem treacherous. The downhill counterpart to the sidestep, the sideslip technique allows easy negotiation of even the steepest hill. Place your skis perpendicular to the slope of the hill; using your knees, put your edges into the hill. Use your poles for balance. By relaxing your knees, the outside edges of the skis will begin to drop and will loosen your grip on the hill. You will begin to slide. If at any time you feel you are sliding too quickly, point your knees back into the hill to slow yourself down.

The technique is a simple one; it also teaches you about knees and their effect on the skis and turning. Figure 4.19 illustrates the slideslip. The knees are pressed into the hill and loosened up to start the sliding of the skis.

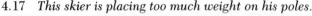

4.17 *This skier is placing too much weight on his poles.*

4.18   *This skier's "V" isn't wide enough.*   4.19   *The downhill sideslip.*

Snowplow

For Alpine skiers, the snowplow is an old friend from the bunny hill. For those new to skiing, the snowplow is a basic technique used by every skier.

The snowplow is the herringbone in reverse: tips together and tails out. Again, your knees should be bent and your upper body relaxed. The poles should be held loosely by your side, with your hands a little forward. As you press your knees forward, you should feel the ski edges dig into the snow. Pressure on the heels will make the tails spread out farther, which will slow you down. Done in unison, these motions will control the rate of descent.

Figure 4.20 shows the body position for the snowplow. The upper body is relaxed, and the knees are bent to provide maximum control for the edges and the speed. If you want to gain speed, straighten out the skis. If you wish to slow down, push out the tails of the skis and angle the edges in more by pushing your knees down.

4.20 *The downhill snowplow.* 4.21 *The half snowplow.*

Half Snowplow

A half snowplow will check a quick descent and help you maintain control without going too slowly. The body position is the same as the snowplow position, but only one ski is in full snowplow position. This technique checks speed, especially in a fast turn, but allows for flexibility (see Figure 4.21).

Parallel Turn

Another old friend from Alpine ski days is the parallel turn. Practice parallel turns on a wide-open packed slope before you attempt them in the woods. Relax your upper body and keep your hands in front of you to keep your weight forward and distributed over the entire foot. As you move down the hill, first plant your pole, then shift the weight from your skis. Now you are in a position to pivot the skis around to head them in a different direction. As you pivot the skis, bring the edges to bear on the slope, keeping the knees angled. Another hint: Your shoulders should always be facing down the hill. This keeps your weight directly over your skis. Figure 4.22 shows a parallel turn being executed.

Step Turn

The step turn uses some of the same moves you learned as you were getting used to your cross-country skis. As you come into the turn, you make a series of quick steps toward the inside of the turn (i.e., the direction in which you are turning).

In Figure 4.23, the skier makes these short, quick steps to bring herself around the turn.

Skate Turn

The most common turn in cross-country skiing is the skate turn. It is difficult to make a sharp turn on the flats using conventional downhill methods unless you've built up a certain amount of speed. Instead the skate turn is used, so named because it is similar to the power motion one uses on ice skates. As you come to a corner, take your outside ski out of the track. Place the ski at an angle to the ski still in the track. Then push off the outside ski as you would a skate. Finally, bring the ski back into the track. As you take this final step with the outside ski, repeat the motion with the inside ski to the inside of the turn. You may have to do this a second or even a third time to negotiate a full turn.

In Figure 4.24 the skier has his ski out of the track and is pushing off it to move himself around the turn.

4.22   *The parallel turn.*

4.23   *The step turn.*

4.24 *The skate turn.*

4.25 *An uncontrolled sideslip.*

4.26 *An ineffective snowplow.*

COMMON MISTAKES

Uncontrolled Sideslip

The knees are not angled toward the hill; as a result, the skis' edges aren't cutting into the hill. The weight of the skier is not directly over the skis (see Figure 4.25).

Ineffective Snowplow

Knees are not angled inward, which means there's no edge control during the descent. There is insufficient spreading of the tails, which renders the "V" in-effective (see Figure 4.26).

Catching an Edge

As with the incorrect snowplow, the knees are not angled into the hill, allowing the outside edges to catch on the turn.

In the Trees

The skier isn't stepping quickly enough. The faster you're going, the quicker you have to step.

VARIATIONS

The marathon skate, the uphill skate, and telemark skiing are all advanced variations of a straight skiing technique.

Marathon Skate

Although rule changes may limit the use of the marathon skate on some parts of the cross-country racecourses, the technique is now used all over the world, especially by elite cross-country skiers, and has changed the face of international racing. It requires immense strength to use it effectively; although it is difficult to execute, it is a useful technique for icy days when your wax wears off, or when the snow is fast and you would like to test it.

The marathon skate is similar to the skate turn. The ski is taken out of the track and, in conjunction with a double pole, provides an extra push down the track. A good marathon skate will increase your speed significantly.

In Figures 4.27a and b the skier lifts the ski out of the track and places the ski at an angle to the other as he begins to "skate" with his ski. He also double poles. He follows through with the double pole and then moves into position for another stroke. Because of the double pole it is easy to rely on your dominant side's strength instead of alternating skis. Train yourself to alternate initially and you won't develop bad habits that will be difficult to break later.

Uphill Skate

This technique requires a great deal of strength, agility, and a well-groomed, wide track. The best way to practice it is to wait for a day when the snow is fast, so you are carrying speed into the hill.

The uphill skate is a faster, more exaggerated herringbone where instead of resting on a stable platform you are gliding on one. As you come to a hill, you skate as you would on ice skates, using your poles for thrust. While you push with your right ski and pole, your left ski is gliding. The left ski is at an angle to prepare for the next push.

As you can see in Figure 4.28, this is an energetic and fast-paced technique.

Telemark Skiing

On a well-packed slope it is possible to telemark with your touring skis, although a pair of telemark skis with their metal edges will facilitate your attempts. The telemark turn is a series of linked turns using the entire ski as a hinged turning device. The key to the turn is to have your weight evenly distributed over the entire ski with the upper body relaxed; if you allow the lead ski to initiate the turn, the rest of the ski will follow.

To assume the classic telemark position, the skier relaxes his upper body and moves his skis so that the tip of the trailing ski meets the leading ski about midway, much like curtsying. The lead ski drives into the turn and brings the skier's entire body around. As in the parallel turn, it is important that the shoulders always face downhill.

4.27a and b   *The marathon skate.*

4.28 *The uphill skate.*

4.29 *Going for it with a high-stepping turn.*

4.30 *If you find yourself going out of control, it's better to fall into a sitting position than tumble.*

FALLING

If you keep practicing, you'll soon be able to pull off a high-stepping turn like the skier in Figure 4.29. But until then, you'll probably take plenty of tumbles. Everybody falls. Make the best of your fall: Control it and fall backward.

In Figure 4.30, the skier has gotten out of control and decided to fall. In this case she simply sits down. Her dignity suffers more than her equipment, but she has made a wise choice.

GETTING UP

Remember, it's not how you fall down, but how you pick yourself up. Once you have fallen, check to see if anything is damaged. If your equipment is okay, move yourself into position so your skis are under you and on the downhill side, perpendicular to the hill. Then raise yourself onto your knees; with both poles in one hand, put them into the snow. Then put your poles into the snow point first on your downhill side. Your back should be to the hill at this point. Grasp the poles at the midsection, and place your other hand on the skis. Now push yourself into a standing position. Shake all the excess snow off (so it doesn't melt and dampen your clothes) and you're ready to go.

As you can see from Figures 4.31a, b, c, and d, standing up is a simple procedure because the heel is not attached to the ski.

4.31a, b, c, and d   *Getting up from a fall.*

4.32 *Taking a lesson from a certified professional will cement your technique.*

4.33 *The author exhibiting dubious technique.*

TAKING A LESSON

Written words are no substitute for a good lesson. A member of the Professional Ski Instructors of America can critique you, answer questions, and offer personalized tips that no book can. I strongly recommend a lesson from a certified professional (see Figure 4.32). PSIA-certified instructors can be found at most of the touring centers in this country.

Failing that, have a friend who skis cross-country watch you; maybe he or she can offer helpful advice (see Figure 4.33). You'll learn a lot and enjoy yourself, too, if you go to a race and watch professionals perform.

CHAPTER FIVE

Cross-Country Skiing for Kids

Bill Koch, Sue Long, and other elite cross-country skiers all get a great deal of enjoyment out of skiing. Finishing a ski marathon gives a real sense of accomplishment to the citizen racer. Skiing the most difficult trail at a cross-country ski center after a week of lessons without falling also brings a sense of pride to a novice cross-country skier. Adults have large twenty-five-cent words for these feelings. Kids just call it fun.

The key to having your child garner the same enjoyment and satisfaction out of skiing that you do is to make it fun. Following are some ideas on how to achieve this goal.

PROTECTION

By its nature, skiing often is cold and can be wet. The combination can dampen the spirit of even the most enthusiastic skiers. Take special precautions to avoid this problem with the younger generation of skiers, where colds can be more dangerous. Make sure they are warmly dressed. When children are beginning to ski they tend to spend a lot of time in the snow itself; dress your child with

(NEW ENGLAND SKI MUSEUM)

this in mind. It is important for children, especially younger children, to wear an outer layer of waterproof material. The snow will slide off instead of melting and dampening other clothes. The under layers can be wool or polypropylene. The former is a better bet because it's cheaper. Important, too, are a good hat and gloves, both made of all-purpose wool.

The more a child skis, the better idea he or she will have about clothing needs. As the day progresses, check that your child still has his or her gloves and hat; injuries from the cold will dampen a child's enthusiasm from the beginning. Younger children will probably have their fill after an hour on skis.

LEARNING

Usually children are eager to learn. Teach them on nonthreatening terrain. A gradual downhill is always fun because they will feel rewarded by being able to glide down after skiing up the hill.

Children will imitate their adult models, so it is important for you to use good technique. Learning the basics requires practice, so the skiing itself should provide your kids with an opportunity to practice and a chance to ski with you.

Provide the kids with an opportunity to practice both uphill and downhill technique. As they become more proficient, a steeper uphill should be incorporated so they can learn to herringbone. These three skills will provide them with a good base. It is important to structure time with kids so they get the most of their time on snow and so they don't get bored.

Games are always fun for kids, and cross-country skiing games will help kids improve the technical aspects of their skiing. Skiing without poles is one of the best methods for teaching balance on cross-country skis. Obstacle courses, follow-the-leader, and hand soccer (have your kids remove their poles and use their hands to play soccer) are all games that give children a better sense of where their skis are in relation to the rest of their body. These sorts of games help them develop a kinesthetic sense of their bodies and cross-country skis.

Follow-the-leader is an all-time favorite. The leader can be you or one of the kids. Use the game as a chance to sneak in a few technique helpers. For instance, have the kids use their double pole or a single-stick motion without moving their legs to get across a flat section. Or make them use their skis to skate from one track to another. The variations are endless. Watch out, though: When the kids lead, you may end up in places only they can get through.

COMPETITION

After your child has skied awhile, he or she may want to try skiing competitively. The United States Ski Association has a wonderful program for kids called the Bill Koch Youth Ski League (see Appendix A for the address). The goal of each of the many clubs all over the United States is to teach kids that cross-country skiing and jumping are fun. The USSA holds races and other events throughout the winter. Write for more information and for the name and address of the club in your area.

CHAPTER SIX

Day Trips, Overnights, and Extended Cross-Country Ski Vacations

"Good morning. It's a beautiful day here in downtown Boston, and we have three inches of snow on the ground. However, our friends to the north were not so lucky. They got six inches."

As you roll over in bed, you wonder if this might not be the perfect day to go cross-country skiing. After all, it is Saturday and the trip to the museum can wait. The pictures will be there next weekend, but the snow may melt. Your new touring skis have been prepped, and the exercises you did this fall have prepared you for the ski trails. But before you load those skis into the car, remember the following.

EAT A GOOD BREAKFAST

For many, breakfast is an underrated meal. As you ski today you may burn up to a thousand calories an hour. Without breakfast, where will your energy come from? Make the bulk of this meal good, complex carbohydrates. They are a great

fuel and burn more slowly than simple carbohydrates such as candy bars. In addition to your pancakes, have an extra bran muffin to give you a little more energy to burn. Have a couple of glasses of water to keep yourself sufficiently hydrated during your ski. This is especially important in the winter. Water is the body's temperature regulator, and a lot of water is lost when you breathe during heavy winter exercise.

CALL AHEAD

A quick phone call to the touring center you are planning to visit can give you not only the conditions of the track but also the road conditions. Cross-country centers are small businesses, and it is possible the area may have closed in the year since you read about it. A call ahead may save you a couple of hours of needless driving.

BRING PLENTY OF CLOTHES

You fall down and soak your clothes, or you may want to go out skiing again after lunch; a dry change of clothes will make you more comfortable. Bring a couple of T-shirts from your summer of road racing so you'll have something dry next to your skin. Staying dry will help prevent unpleasant midwinter colds.

PACK MORE CARBOHYDRATES

Now's the time to have that extra piece of bread without worrying about it showing up on your waist. Instead it will provide energy to ski, and you'll burn it off. Don't forget to bring in your thermos something warm to drink.

DON'T FORGET

Your wax kit, emergency kit, and all your equipment. My personal experience tells me to double-check everything (I had to ski the most important race of my career on someone else's poles because I forgot mine). Your backpack should have a few essentials besides your lunch: the trail map and extra clothes, especially if you are planning a ski longer than an hour or two.

Remember:

- a standard first-aid kit
- extra food
- extra sunglasses
- knife
- compass
- space blanket (a lightweight blanket made of reflective material)
- extra binding and screws
- duct tape
- epoxy and wire
- candle and flashlight

Once you have arrived at the trailhead, be sure to get a map so you know where you are going. If there is a trail fee, pay it. Not doing so is called "theft of services," and cross-country ski center owners do prosecute. Signing out and back in at the end of the day means the touring center can keep track of its patrons during the day. They will do a final sweep when the center closes, but if they don't know you're still out there, they can't know to look for you.

WARM UP AND DOWN

Warming up helps prepare you for a full day of skiing (see page 118). Start out slowly so your muscles can get used to the exercise, particularly after a long ride, or on the first day of your ski season.

After the day is over, change your shirt, and warm down with a hot drink. If you are going to drive, make that drink nonalcoholic. Alcohol will make you especially light-headed after a hard day of exercise.

Once at home, be sure to wipe off your skis, put your boots in a warm (but not hot) place to dry, and take a sauna or hot bath; you deserve it.

LONGER TRAVEL

Sports vacations are becoming more and more popular. These trips may be a weekend cross-country ski trip to a cozy New England inn such as Blueberry Hill in Goshen, Vermont, or a week-long trip out to Busterback Lodge in Ketchum, Idaho. Both places offer a wide range of skiing activities. Like one-day trips, these trips are the most fun and rewarding when well planned.

When planning a ski weekend or week-long cross-country ski retreat, consider the following:

The Snow Conditions at That Time of Year

Snow conditions in northern New England in early April can be disappointing; in early January or late December, western skiing can be bitterly cold. Find out when the best times are.

Skis: Renting or Transporting?

This depends on your capacity to carry skis through airports and on what's available in the rental shop where you're headed. If you are using a racing ski now, you won't find much to suit you. On the other hand, if you're just beginning, most rentals shops should be able to suit you up. Call ahead to be sure of your options.

Lessons

Lessons are a great way to improve your technique and will help you get more out of your stay. But don't be afraid to go off on your own; you'll learn by your mistakes and attempts as well.

Nightly Entertainment

Most ski resorts offer entertainment, but in many cases you will want to sleep after a vigorous day on the trails. Still, if the conditions are poor and you're not able to ski, entertainment may be important.

Following are names of and information about some of the classic cross-country ski resorts in the United States. Many of the resorts listed in Appendix D offer the same services, but this list represents some of my favorite vacation spots.

Blueberry Hill
Goshen, VT 05733
802-247-6535
A quaint country inn in northern Vermont and famous for its fine French cuisine. Owner and host Tony Clark is a remarkable combination of ski teacher and cook.

Jackson Ski Touring Foundation
Jackson, NH 03846
603-383-9355
This community cross-country ski resort, tucked in the beautiful White Mountains, offers over one hundred kilometers of skiing among some of the finest inns and restaurants in New England.

Bretton Woods
Route 302
Bretton Woods, NH 03575
603-278-5000
A full-service resort, including Alpine and cross-country ski trails as well as fine eateries. It's the summer home of the Mount Washington Hotel. The cover photo for this book was shot at this resort.

Busterback Ranch
Star Rte.
Ketchum, ID 83340
208-774-2217
Tucked away in the backcountry high above the famous Sun Valley resort, the Busterback Resort offers cross-country skiing for all levels of expertise from beginner trails to guided backcountry telemark trips in a rustic setting.

Royal Gorge Cross-Country Ski
   Center
P.O. Box 178
Soda Springs, CA 95728
916-426-3871
Park your car, load your equipment onto the sleds, and be whisked into a secluded lodge for three days of great French cooking and good times. Don't be concerned if you have to walk downstairs to get to the top floor of the lodge. Thirty feet of snow is the norm.

Lone Mountain Ranch
P.O. Box 145
Big Sky, MT 59716
406-995-4644
The United States Biathlon Team trains here for two weeks every year because the snow is great and the food is better. Even though they train twice a day, these athletes still gain weight because the food is so great. The skiing and hospitality measure up as well.

Telemark Lodge
Cable, WI 54821
715-798-3811
This is the home of the American Birkebeiner, which is the largest cross-country race in the United States, with some eight thousand participants from all over the world. Telemark Lodge has some of the finest cross-country ski trails in the country. Expert trails are some of the toughest found, and the beginner trails have great views.

C Lazy U Ranch
P.O. Box 378
Granby, CO 80446
303-887-3344
A family place in the heart of Colorado ski country, the C Lazy U has it all—great skiing, great food, and hospitality.

Craftsbury Nordic Ski Center
Craftsbury Common, VT 05827
802-586-2514
One of the best places in the
Northeast for early snow; they have
excellent tracks. There is training
available for elite skiers, and lessons
for beginners.

Snow Mountain Ranch
P.O. Box 558
Granby, CO 80446
303-887-2152
The YMCA has created a cross-
country skier's mecca in the middle
of the Colorado Rockies. In addition
to great skiing of its own, Snow
Mountain Ranch is a short drive to
nine of the best cross-country ski
areas in Colorado. This is a full-
service operation with meals and
lodging.

Mt. Batchelor Nordic Sports Center
P.O. Box 1031
Bend, OR 97701
503-382-2442
Located at the bottom of the famous
Mt. Batchelor alpine ski area, which
has catered to downhill skiers for
years, the Nordic Sports Center has
tapped Bob Matthews and his crew
to turn their expertise to cross-
country ski trails. Long seasons and
a quality setting are the two
hallmarks of this center. In May the
U.S. Ski Team can be found here
skiing on the late spring snow.

Sherman Hollow Ski Touring
   Center
R.D. 1, P.O. Box 175
Richmond, VT 05477
802-434-2057
This resort is one of my personal
favorites because of the obvious
care the owners have taken with all
aspects of the cross-country ski
experience. The trails are well-
groomed, especially the night loop,
and the dinners prepared in the
lodge are a delight to the tired and
hungry skier.

CHAPTER SEVEN

Training and Conditioning

As I sit down to write this chapter, the weather outside is cold and gray, but I can feel the snow in the air. Later today I probably will go downstairs to get my skis out of storage in the basement; then it will be upstairs to the attic to dust off my ski clothes. As I think about getting out my ski equipment, my thoughts turn to the preparation of another piece of equipment, my body.

For elite athletes, training is a year-round endeavor. The Gunde Svans, Marie Hannieliemins, Bill Kochs, Sharon Firths, and Sue Longs of the cross-country ski world train for skiing year round. Their training consists of roller skiing, marathon skating, slide boarding, running with poles, and weight work-outs. The list goes on from there. They are training either to maintain their position as the best, or to improve their status in world rankings. These goals require the dedication of year-round training. However, the vast majority of us use skiing as only one of many physical outlets.

For those who don't have the luxury of intensive year-round training or on-snow training seven months of the year, cross-country skiing can be done only occasionally in the winter to complement our other physical endeavors. Those may include running, aerobic dance, bicycling, roller skating, weight lifting, tennis, or rowing. Or maybe you have come to cross-country skiing through the back door. You started skiing last winter, and it's the first serious physical activity you have ever done. Realizing what terrible shape you were in, you decided to start a training program so that next year won't be so bad.

As with any new physical fitness program, before you embark upon it you should have a complete physical examination by a doctor. Many of the exercises in the following program may present new strains to your body that could cause problems. For example, roller skiing, a direct simulation of cross-country skiing on snow, may seem easy on the body. However, it could result in tendinitis of the elbows caused by the shock of the pole going into the asphalt. As a precautionary method, get a physical examination and ask your doctor if he or she thinks you're up to a new fitness program, and if so, how strenuous it could be.

WARM-UP

Those of us without the luxury of a garage get into our cars on cold winter mornings to find that the seats are stiff, the steering wheel is cold, and starting the engine requires prayers and incantations over the ignition. When the engine finally does roar to life, the heater first blows cold air, and the engine is tentative and sluggish. Finally, as the defroster clears the windows, the car is able to move.

In many ways your body is similar to your car. You may have the luxury of keeping it in the warm garage of your bed, and your heater may blow warm air as you breathe on your fingers, but all that aside, you still need to warm up before you dash out to ski.

Warming up is one of the most important parts of a workout. The muscles and joints need to be warm to work to full efficiency, and more important, to prevent injury. A well-warmed-up muscle transports blood better and gives greater range of motion. Squeeze your right hand right now into a fist as hard as you can, and hold that for fifteen seconds. Then slowly move your fingers into an open hand; the tightness you experience is similar to what your muscles feel after they have been in bed for the night, or sitting at your desk for a regular workday.

A warm-up allows the muscle to move from a state of relative inactivity to one of suppleness and peak efficiency. Because you are moving the muscle from relative inactivity to serious activity the warm-up must be complete. Each warm-up should start with a period of light movement. If you are going to go for a ski, stretching indoors in your ski clothes is a good idea. The stretches below (see Figure 7.1) are recommended ones that can be supplemented with others from *The Complete Book of Stretching* by Robert Anderson (see the Selected Bibliography).

Do these stretches slowly, with no bouncing. Bouncing during stretching can lead to pulled muscles. Breathing during the stretch is important. For the first two thirds of a stretch, stretch until you feel a pulling on the muscle being stretched. Hold the stretch. For the final third, stretch until you feel the tightness of the muscle being worked. The entire stretching routine should be done slowly. Remember that it is important to breathe during the entire stretch.

Once you feel stretched out, do a few sit-ups, push-ups, or any exercises to get the heart rate up. This starts the inner muscle warm-up. When the core of the muscle is warm, you are ready to ski efficiently.

Once outside, do a few warm-ups on your skis. These will help you adjust to the cold outdoors and to your skis.

Once you have finished the outdoor stretches (these should be similar to some of the ones you did inside), move down the trail slowly. Don't blast out of the starting gate—you run the risk of injury and of tiring yourself out too early. Start slowly and prepare yourself, whether it's for an hour-long ski tour, an all-day ski, or a marathon race. The engine needs to be well warmed to be efficient.

Warm up year round. No matter what the season, the muscles and joints need to be warm to perform at peak efficiency and to prevent injury. Unless your muscles are adequately stretched, you could be running the risk of injury.

TYPES OF TRAINING

The following workouts are used by elite and citizen skiers alike. The workouts have many variations and in their simplest form are the basis for a complete training program.

Long Distance

To get your body ready for a marathon or even an all-day ski tour, you must put in long hours beforehand, and gradually build up your endurance for longer and longer periods of exertion. A good house cannot be built without a solid foundation.

7.1 *Ten different warm-up stretches. Do these slowly and without bouncing.*

If you've never trained before, you might begin with an hour of brisk walking on a Sunday afternoon. If you're already a runner, make a long run on Sunday part of your weekly regimen. An elite cross-country skier would probably roller ski for three hours, or speed hike for six hours in mountainous terrain.

Walk, bike, roller ski, swim, do aerobic dance, or run. Your goal is continuous physical exertion that will increase your heart rate to between 100 and 120 beats per minute. This rate means that you are building your aerobic capacity and training your body to operate at that level for long periods. The initial duration of your workout depends on your previous condition and could last from one to four hours. If your workout schedule is built around a week, the long-distance workout should be done once a week. Don't overexert yourself. Let your body adjust gradually.

Middle Distance

A shortened workout time with increased intensity is called a "cruising workout" by elite racers. They don't hold themselves back, as they do during a long-distance workout, or push themselves, as with an interval workout. Middle-distance workouts allow them to cruise at an even pace with their heart rates between 120 and 150 beats per minute. At this pace they can enjoy the fruits of their labor on the fast downhills and on the easy lope up the hills.

The purpose of this workout is to go at a faster pace than a normal-distance workout and to use the muscles at a higher rate. This workout is the best time to concentrate on transitions in ski terrain and technique, which are important to good and efficient performance. A middle-distance workout can also be used to recover from a long workout, helping to shake the long-distance slows (these happen when you train at the same slow speed every day and thus train yourself to move slowly) "out" of the system.

Again, the length of the workout depends on your current level of conditioning. A beginner skier should keep it slow and short; a well-conditioned athlete probably will want to stay out longer.

Biking, running, sculling, or aerobic dance are all adequate to raise your heart rate, but roller skiing or cross-country skiing are the best. The middle-distance workouts should be done two or three times a week. Don't make these workouts the main staple of your workout menu; they're easy, but adjusting to the higher speeds for races of the same length or longer will be difficult. You will have trained your body to move at a certain speed for a specific length of time.

Speed Workouts

There has been a move away from a steady diet of long-distance and middle-distance workouts to ones designed to help the athlete move faster. The move has been controversial, but one thing is certain: To ski fast, you have to ski efficiently. These workouts are designed to teach the athlete how to move quickly and efficiently (as well as offering conditioning benefits) over the distance of the race.

There are three main types of speed workouts: leg speed workouts, interval workouts, and tempo-race pace workouts. Before you begin an intense workout, be sure to warm up. Speed increases the chance of injury.

LEG-SPEED WORKOUTS

Leg-speed workouts are short-distance (one hundred to two hundred meters) exercises done repeatedly. By limiting the body to distances of one hundred to two hundred meters, muscles move more quickly, yet anaerobic energy is not drained. Begin by marking out a two-hundred-meter section of a track. Ski the section as quickly and efficiently as possible in one direction; then, after a brief rest, do the section again, in reverse. Don't be concerned if you feel uncoordinated during the first few workouts; remember, you are retraining your muscles. Keep track of your times over the sections and, as you work out more often, your times will drop.

Your leg-speed workout can be incorporated into your middle-distance workout and should be done at least once a week. The number of repeats you can do will reflect the state of your conditioning, as will the distance. If two hundred meters isn't comfortable, try one hundred meters, or work in only one direction. (A more detailed explanation of these workouts and other training information can be found in the United States Ski Coaches' *A Basic Guide to Competitive Cross-Country Skiing, Parts One and Two;* see the Selected Bibliography.)

INTERVAL WORKOUTS

Interval workouts are intense and can last from one to fifteen minutes. They are designed to train the body to work at high energy output. Interval workouts are more stressful to your body than the majority of other workouts you will do.

Interval workouts can be as formal as skiing a measured distance repeatedly on a track, or as informal as sprinting up the hills during a bike ride. After each period of intense work, rest while your body recovers. Recovery time can be calculated by the amount of time it takes for your pulse to drop to 120 beats per minute. The workout ends when your body is exhausted and you cannot complete the recovery before the next repeat.

When biking for your interval workout, you might observe the following regimen: Choose a course that reflects your conditioning; then, after warming up, sprint up the hills, rest on the downhills, and cruise easily on the flats. You should recover completely before you sprint up the next hill.

Interval workouts should be done at least once a week, in the later part of the training cycle. This workout is tough and should be followed by a good warm-down (see page 140). The warm-down will help you derive full benefit from the next day's exercise. Many books on running discuss intervals or the Swedish "speed play" if you want more information on this form of training.

TEMPO-RACE PACE WORKOUTS

During tempo-race pace workouts, you simulate the racing situation but without the extra conditions. There are no cheering crowds, no perfectly groomed tracks, and no encouraging coaches. It is a tough workout.

The object is to attune your body to the strain of racing. It's important for athletes to listen to what their bodies tell them. Don't force the action, breathe, and relax, but pull out the stops. Tempo-race pace will help make racing second nature to your body.

You begin by measuring out a typical racecourse length, perhaps five kilometers. Now ski, bike, or run this course as quickly as you can. The first time, you may want to do it only once, but as you get better, you may want to ski two loops. Be sure to time yourself so you can keep track of your improvement. It's best to roller ski or ski the workout; the closer the simulation, the better. This workout should be done once a week throughout the year, particularly during the latter part of the summer and in the winter when you're not racing.

CROSS-TRAINING

Many of you came to cross-country skiing via another sport. Because of time and location, skiing may not be your primary sport but one that will complement your main interest. If you are a biker, riding the rollers during the winter is not only boring, but your competitive urge may not be fulfilled. Cross-country skiing may be the perfect companion sport for you. In addition, you may strengthen muscles not normally used in bicycling.

Cross-training is a term coined in the booming sport of triathloning. Athletes found that a tri-diet helped them to become stronger in other sports. It is generally accepted that triathlon runners suffer fewer of the leg injuries that plague those whose sole form of physical conditioning is running. The extra doses of swimming and biking make them more completely fit.

As a complementary sport, cross-country skiing can help achieve the same cross-training benefits. In preparing for the transition from your primary sport to cross-country skiing, it's important to realize that cross-country skiing is an aerobic sport like running, biking, swimming, sculling, or aerobic dance. However, like those sports, skiing has its specific demands. For instance, unlike running, cross-country skiing requires significant use of the upper body. Elite cross-country skiers generate through their arms and back as much as 50 percent of the power used to move down the track. Many runners, bikers, and walkers have found after their first skiing experiences that they had muscles in their arms they never thought existed. The following activities are excellent complements to cross-country skiing.

Walking

Many of us walk, but few people realize it is becoming a national passion. To help in your conditioning for cross-country skiing, as the weather turns colder, walk with a quicker tempo to get your heart rate up, and with a more pronounced stride to simulate a diagonal stride (see Figure 7.2). To strengthen the arms, carry a pair of hand weights while you are walking. Pull on an Exer-Genie (see page 131) for fifteen to twenty minutes three times a day. If you walk farther once a week than you normally do in that time, you'll gradually build your distance base.

Swimming

Swimming, like cross-country skiing, is a "soft" sport because it is easy on the joints (see Figure 7.3). But, unlike skiing, you depend mostly on your arms for propulsion. If swimming is your primary activity, consider spending about twenty minutes every other day on a stationary bicycle. This helps build the quadriceps and hamstrings, which won't be adapted to the demands of skiing through swimming.

7.2 *A vigorous walk is an excellent preparation for cross-country skiing.*

7.3 *Swimming will help build your upper arms.*

Running

Running develops your leg muscles but won't build arm strength. A weight program using the specific exercises would stand you in good stead during the long winter tour. You'll also have faster running times (see Figure 7.4).

If you are a serious runner, add more hills to your workouts. Add natural interval workouts as well: Run quickly up the hills and slowly down them (let natural momentum carry you).

Racquet Sports

If you look at a professional tennis player, it looks as if someone took one of his or her arms and inflated it. In addition, the player's legs must be adapted to a stop-and-start game. However, the transition from tennis player to skier isn't difficult because good conditioning is basic to both sports. A weight program involving specific exercises plus a little running will help ease the transition to cross-country skiing.

7.4 *Running will help build your leg muscles.*

7.5 *Bicycling and cross-country skiing use many of the same muscle groups.*

7.6 *Rowing is one of the best cardiovascular workouts.*

Biking

At first glance, biking would seem a distant relative of cross-country skiing. However, both bikers and skiers encounter natural intervals in the terrain and must work hard on the uphills and then glide on the downhills. The downward pressure on the pedal by the cyclist is similar to the kick of the cross-country skier. To facilitate the transition, add a little weight workout with some running (to keep the groin stretched and less susceptible to strain) and you have the perfect complement to cross-country skiing (see Figure 7.5).

Rowing

Rowing is probably one of the best exercises to prepare for cross-country skiing (see Figure 7.6), for unlike biking and running, you use both arms and legs rowing. Few if any changes in your basic rowing program need be made for an easy transition to snow. However, as with cycling, I recommend stretching as well as a little running to help prevent strain in the groin area.

Aerobic Dance

Aerobic dance has all the right components to prepare you for cross-country skiing. Weight work with the specific exercises I have listed will focus conditioning further. Many aerobic dance classes use hand weights, but you'll need to incorporate the specific movements of cross-country skiing into your routines.

Routines that call for a lot of bouncing make aerobic dancers susceptible to shin splints and other overuse injuries. Cross-country skiing will strengthen the leg muscles and help prevent these injuries.

Triathlon

Skiing is the perfect off-season sport for the triathlete who is forced to cut back on running or biking because of the snow. There are few adjustments to make because the upper body has strength from swimming, while the lower body has been readied through running and cycling. A swimmer's shoulders will benefit from the single and double poles of cross-country skiing.

TRAINING FOR THE UPPER BODY

Training the muscles beforehand circumvents the stiffness that may accompany a first-time ski. There are many ways to prepare your upper body: swimming, pull-ups, a weight program, rowing, or using a roller board (see page 131). However, the key to any strengthening program for cross-country skiing is the SAID principle.

SAID stands for Specific Adaption to Imposed Demands—that is, adapting your body specifically for the demands that will be placed upon it. Doing fifty pull-ups a day will strengthen your upper body, but this is not a good use of time because the muscles strengthened may not be of any help when, for example, you double pole (although if you are a rock climber, it will help a lot). The following exercises are aimed at developing muscles used during cross-country skiing and can easily be added to your current exercise program. In many cases they will add to your overall physical strength, which will also enhance performance.

The following exercises are designed to strengthen your single pole and your double pole. In addition, there are suggested exercises designed to improve overall body strength.

7.7   *The dip.*

7.8   *The back raise.*

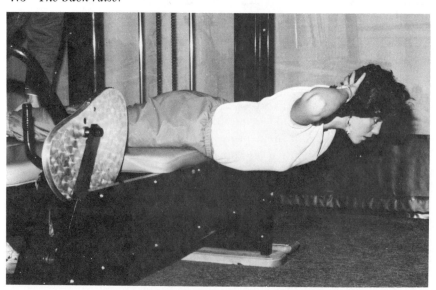

Sit-Ups

The sit-up is an old standby. Place your hands across the chest to remove the temptation to jerk your head up. Doing sit-ups while anchoring your feet and bending your knees is comparable to a double pole movement.

If doing sit-ups on flat ground is too easy, try the inclined plane. The next step in difficulty is to do sit-ups while holding a weight to your chest.

Dips

Another old standby, which has a number of variations, is the dip (see Figure 7.7). When lowering yourself, dip just past the ninety-degree angle formed by your arm and then lift yourself back up. If this exercise becomes too easy, put on a daypack with about ten pounds, or have a child sit on your back.

Back Raises

This exercise strengthens the back muscles that are important to all phases of the diagonal stride (see Figure 7.8). Don't raise yourself past level or you'll place unnecessary strain on your back. If you use a weight, hold it tightly next to your chest to make the exercise more difficult. Placing the weight on the back of your neck may cause undue strain on the lower back.

Exer-Genie

This friction rope device is popular with members of the United States Cross-Country Ski Team because it's portable as well as functional. Use it to simulate poling. It can also be used for strength or cardiovascular workouts. See Appendix B under training devices for Exer-Genies. They cost about forty dollars.

Rollerboard

When Marty Hall found this device at an East German training camp back in the early seventies, he brought back plans to his teams. Simple to make, the rollerboard provides the perfect workout for your double pole. The rollerboard can be used lying down or kneeling (see Figure 7.9).

Rollerboards are easy to construct. You will need one 4′ × 8′ sheet of ¾-inch plywood, twenty-four feet of half-inch molding, four non-swivel dolly

7.9 *The rollerboard.*

wheels, two fourteen-foot pieces of two-by-four, a piece of heavy-duty rope, and
a piece of four-foot webbing.

Out of the plywood cut a 2′ × 8′ piece, a 2′ × 4′ piece, and cut a twelve-
foot section off of each of the two-by-fours. Now nail the two-by-four to the plywood so that you have a twelve-foot ramp. This is what you will be sliding up
and down on. With the leftover two-by-four place cross-pieces under the ramp
to help strengthen your roller board. Place the molding along the sides of the
ramp. This will keep your sled (see below) on track as you move up and down
the ramp. The ramp is now complete.

Take the rest of the plywood and cut yourself a piece that is approximately
2′ × 2½′: this will serve as your sled. Place the non-swivel dolly wheels on each
of the corners. Be sure the wheels are placed at least 1½ inches away from the
edge of the board. This allows the sled to fit easily on the ramp. Now attach
the rope to one end of the ramp so there is equal length on both sides.
Attach the nylon webbing to the ropes in loops like a ski pool strap. Now hop
on and do your workout.

7.10 *The bench press.*

OVERALL STRENGTH BUILDERS THROUGH WEIGHT TRAINING

Whether you use Nautilus, Universal, Cam II, or free weights for your overall strength program, use them in conjunction with the ski specific exercises I've just described. A couple of strongly recommended exercises follow.

Bench Press

The bench press (see Figure 7.10) is a great strength-building exercise for the chest muscles and the triceps (poling muscles).

Leg Press

This exercise builds leg muscles that provide the power needed to propel yourself up hills.

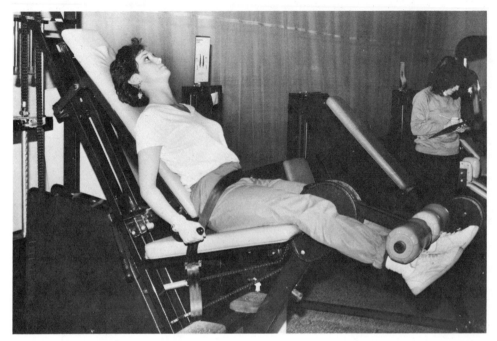

7.11   *The knee extension machine.*

Lat Double Pole

Wrap a towel around the bar on the Lat machine and pull down. The exercise is an exact replica of the double-pole motion in skiing.

Knee Extension Front and Back

The knee extension machine (see Figure 7.11) helps strengthen the quadricep and other muscles around the knee that help drive the ski down the track. In addition, this machine builds muscles to prevent knee injury.

The back knee extension machine helps strengthen the hamstring, which provides quadriceps balance on downhills and in the gliding phase.

A reputable health club or your local "Y" will have personnel who can design a comprehensive weight program for you (see Figure 7.12a and b). However, it is important to remember to incorporate dips, sit-ups, back-ups, the Exer-Genie, Lat double poles, and double pole machines into any strength program to practice the SAID principle.

7.12a and b *The Nautilus triceps and pull-up machines can be part of your strength-building weight program.*

TOWARD A PHILOSOPHY OF TRAINING

How much? How little? When? How come? All these are questions about training. To a point, each training program must be individually adapted. Yet for more serious skiers there will be certain training musts. An Olympic hopeful has to put in a certain amount of distance, speed, tempo, technique, and strength training, not to mention mental imagery ski preparation (a sophisticated method of psychological training involving imagining yourself skiing perfectly).

What about the person who does not have Olympic aspirations, or even racing aspirations? No matter who or what your goals are, each of us has something in mind when we jump into the pool, step onto the mat for aerobics, or put on headphones for a two-mile jog. I come from a large, mostly unathletic family—that was, until a year ago. My mother, who used to run only when mice attacked, now runs a mile a day—to the Rolling Stones, no less. My sister, who considered opening a car door a strenuous workout, now rhapsodizes about her daily swimming. She's known as a pool bore. My brother, a former college lacrosse player, now plans to run a hundred-mile race and a marathon, and to enter Hawaii's iron-man Triathlon contest in the next three years. Their goals include: losing weight; good health; finishing the iron-man; and, in my mother's case, "maintaining the hearts in my calves, and maybe beating Mrs. Goldman in the annual Auburn two-mile road race."

Before you begin a program of any type, set a realistic goal; this places training into a framework, which helps you gauge the training's importance. If the goal of your program is to have fun and lose some weight along the way, you don't have to run on an icy day in late February. But if your goal is to make the United States Ski Team, you'll want to get some kilometers under your belt. Once your goal has been established, you can begin training.

Training is much like building a fire. You have to start with small twigs and paper to get it burning, not smother a spark with huge logs. As the fire gets going and starts to burn, you can put on bigger logs to build and maintain the heat. If my mother the jogger had set a goal of five miles for her first day out, she would have gotten discouraged when she could only run one-half mile. She might have burned her running shoes and headed back for the easy chair. Instead, she began by walking. Build a training base. Don't end up defeated before reaching your goals.

Olympic aspirations aside, it's important to have fun in cross-country skiing. Learning to ski well and to condition yourself will help you enjoy your tour through the winter woods.

TRAINING PRINCIPLES

When physically preparing yourself for any endeavor, a few basic rules will make the experience more fruitful and enjoyable.

- Specific Adaption to Imposed Demands (SAID). If you're training for cross-country skiing, it is important to teach your muscles the exact movements that will be required of them out on the trail.
- Use It or Lose It. Some say you start losing it after a day without exercise, some say you go back to the level of conditioning you had before you began to exercise. Either way, you lose your conditioning if you don't maintain it.
- Individual Response. Everyone responds to programs differently. If a 6-foot, 180-pound man ran ten miles a day every day, there's a good chance he would be injured within the month, whereas a 6-foot, 150-pound man could withstand the stress.
- Vary Your Workout. Whether it is a full-time occupation or part of your daily routine, your training should be varied. Include hard and easy days; avoid overtraining; look at the quality, not the quantity of the exercise. The most important part of training is to begin it early in the seasonal cycle. If you are getting ready for an early-winter ski touring trip in Yellowstone National Park, you can start training in September, but if you plan to follow the Great American Ski Chase this winter, you should start training in the spring.
- Train Every Day. Conditioning should be part of your daily schedule. Prepare for the individual sports. Don't surprise your body. If cross-country skiing is a complementary sport for you, you'll want to make some seasonal adjustments to your other sport to enhance your next cross-country experience.

The step beyond these subtle changes in your current program is aerobic exercises specific to cross-country skiing, not simply extensions of an existing program. It is possible to use these different training methods instead of your current program on a given day. For example, instead of swimming one day, go roller skiing, or hike with poles.

Hiking with Poles

This is the perfect exercise for anyone who hikes, walks, or does a sport that doesn't incorporate stride, such as biking or rowing. The next time you go out for a walk or a hike, take a pair of your old cross-country ski poles. As you hike, imitate the cross-country ski stride. Use your arms as you go uphill, as well as good diagonal technique. This is specific training.

If you would like to take this one step further, you can run with poles and do natural interval workouts on the hills. Or you can do hill running with poles. Select a hill and stride up it; use the downhill for recovery.

Roller Skiing

Roller skis are about three feet long. They come with two or three wheels and are designed to simulate the movement and technique of cross-country skiing. They are the perfect off-season training device. Not only do they feel like skis, but also they provide the same conditioning (see Figure 7.13).

However, these skis have drawbacks. Asphalt is not as forgiving as snow.

7.13   *Roller skiing.*

In fact, a low-speed crash on roller skis can leave a good part of your epidermis on the highway. To avoid such unfortunate accidents, first scout the road ahead of time so you know where all the downhills are. (If the downhill is steep, walk down it. There is little training effect from rolling downhill.) Second, pick a well-paved little-traveled road. Motorists won't know to watch for you. They are used to seeing runners and cyclists, but roller skiers are unusual. Finally, if you decide to use the skis a lot, have a coach watch your technique so you don't develop bad habits.

Marathon Skates

The newest wrinkle in training is the marathon skate (see Figure 7.14). These skates were used by speed skaters and hockey players to develop their technique. Throw in a pair of poles and you have a perfect way to practice your marathon skate. Unlike on their counterpart the roller skate, the wheels on the marathon skate are set in a single row.

However, marathon skates are costly ($140), and unless you plan to use them exclusively, as the elite racers do, the money would be better spent on a good pair of roller skis.

The same cautions apply to marathon skating as to roller skiing. Be careful out there.

7.14 *Marathon skating.*

Indoor Cross-Country Ski Simulators

The growth of cross-country skiing in the past few years has spawned a number of indoor ski simulators. The machines are found in many of the health clubs and are popular with people who want to condition both the lower and upper portions of their body and who want to exercise indoors.

In theory the machines are a good idea. However, with one exception (Nordic Ski Track), they do not simulate the cross-country diagonal movement closely enough. To make the Nordic Ski Track work correctly, good technique is a must. These machines cost about $470 per unit.

See Appendix B for the addresses of roller ski and marathon skate manufacturers. Ski simulators are also listed there. They cost in the four to six hundred dollar range.

WARM-DOWN

Exercise, especially hard or intense exercise, produces metabolic by-products. An intense interval workout, for instance, will produce excess lactic acid. Warming down while you make your recovery will remove many of these by-products. Many of us have experienced stiffness after a first-time ski or a hard workout. A good warm-down will prevent some of this stiffness, which we may attempt to pass off as old age.

A good warm-down consists of light jogging or easy skiing after the main section of workout to help the heart rate return to normal. After you have taken off your skis and moved indoors, relax with a warm drink and some light stretching exercises. Warming down may be the most important part of your exercise regimen because it helps prevent injuries and speeds recovery from exercise. If you are a sometime skier, it is important that you be able to ski whenever you have the chance.

DIET

Most Americans, if they eat three square meals a day, consume all the vitamins they need. If you feel you need insurance, take a daily multiple-vitamin capsule. Women, because of their menstrual cycle, should take a supplement with iron.

Americans in general eat too much fat and cholesterol. If you can cut down on fatty foods and whole-milk dairy products, you will be healthier. You'll also cut out some unneeded calories.

Complex carbohydrates are better for you than simple sugars. An apple is better for you than a candy bar and will provide more energy on the next ski tour.

Most Americans also consume too much protein. You need less than one hundred grams of protein a day. If you are going out for a day-long tour or hike, French toast or pancakes will provide more usable energy than a steak. Energy is easier to convert from carbohydrates than from proteins and fats.

Drink more water than usual before you go out on the trail. If you are properly hydrated you will feel better and will recover from exercise more quickly.

To lose weight, you have to increase your output of energy (calories) and/or decrease your intake of calories. Unused calories will be turned to fat. Experience tells us it is easier to walk more than to try to give up our midmorning Danish. But how about taking a walk or running longer if you are going to eat that Danish? Better yet, run more and give up the Danish. With proper diet and nutrition, you'll not only get more out of your cross-country tours, you'll also find you have more energy for all your other activities. See the Selected Bibliography for a listing of diet and nutrition books.

CHAPTER EIGHT

Racing

If you've been touring and are feeling competitive or you think it's time to test yourself at a longer distance, maybe you should enter your first race. Each year 40 percent of the contestants in the American Birkebeiner's race field are first time racers (see Figure 8.1). People train all year just to ski the fifty-five-kilometer race from Hayward, Wisconsin, to Telemark, Wisconsin, with eight thousand others. (If after your first race you're hooked, authors Marty Hall, Bob Woodward, and John Caldwell have excellent information about cross-country ski racing (see the Selected Bibliography for titles and further descriptions).

Once you've decided to race, choose your first race carefully. Short races are less challenging but are easier to train for. A long race will challenge both heart and mind. You can even participate in skiing's marathon madness (see Figure 8.2).

The United States Ski Association sanctions races of all distances throughout the country. Membership in the USSA not only brings you this complete list of events, it also keeps you tuned into the U.S. cross-country skiing world.

With the help of sponsors, the USSA underwrites development programs to assist upcoming skiers and helps them to reach their potential whether they're skiing locally, nationally, or internationally. In addition, the USSA works hard to raise the quality of ski racing in this country. See Appendix A for the address of the USSA office in your area.

Let's say for the sake of discussion you have chosen a short race for your first race. When I say short, I mean the distance is less than fifteen kilometers. Your goal in both short and long races should be to finish. Placing in your age category or winning may be too high a goal the first time out. In any case, opt for a race that has a mass start—i.e., a race where everyone begins at the same time. Compared with interval-start races, where racers leave the gate every thirty seconds (sometimes two at a time), mass start races offer the opportunity to ski with people of your ability.

If you are going to race in a short race, a couple of days should be devoted to skiing a distance just farther than your racecourse. Ski it comfortably and don't push yourself; the adrenaline will take care of that on the day of the actual race. Longer-distance races may pose more of a problem. Trying to ski the entire distance every day in training will burn you out. Instead, when training for a longer race, do long-distance workouts for two or three hours a couple of days a month. These long-distance workouts will form the backbone of your training for the race. In addition to these workouts, continue to ski whenever you can, or use roller skis, and keep up your regular training program.

Once you've begun to train, attend to the "administrative" side of the race. Be sure you know when the entry application is due. (Entry fees in the most popular races are graduated, so the sooner you send in your money, the less you pay to race.) The day before the race, call the race headquarters and double-check the time, place, and distance. This is also a good time to check your wax kit and your equipment. Is it time to replace that worn pole strap? Do you need wax? Are your bindings loose? If there's no change predicted in the weather, it may be a good time to put glide wax on your skis. Scrape the skis once and place them outside. Then check your equipment again to be sure everything is in "racing shape."

Your meals the day before a race should be high in carbohydrates. If it's a longer race, consider a diet high in carbohydrates for the three or four days before the race. This will ensure energy for the long race. After you have waxed, eaten, and fussed, it is a good time to relax before going to bed. I find beer helps me relax before sleeping.

One last point: It would be impossible to drink too much water before a

8.1   *The American Birkebeiner is one of the most popular races.* (Telemark)

8.2 *Racing is a good way to test yourself at longer distances.* (SAMUEL P. OSBORNE)

8.3 *Fueling up during the race.* (SAMUEL P. OSBORNE)

race. Hydrating yourself not only helps protect against the cold but also helps keep the fluids flowing in the body.

When setting your alarm clock, remember that you need to be at the race at least one and a half hours before the start. Once you're there, check in, pick up your bib, and double-check the starting time. (Some of the larger races distribute bibs the night before the race to eliminate last-minute confusion.) If you haven't already done so, head out to the course to figure out what wax to use. Check with others to pin down the correct wax. After you have made last-minute adjustments and are happy with the wax you've chosen, take a drink of water and remember to perform your prerace constitutional. Then begin your warm-up. Do a few stretching exercises, paying particular attention to the groin and back areas. Once you've stretched, put on your skis and take a short ski. Ski easily at first, but finish off with a few short bursts to get your muscles well warmed up.

After you finish your warm-up, take off your warm-up suit and move to the starting line. If you're skiing in a marathon race, be sure to carry extra wax and an extra hat in your beltpack. Choose your starting position according to your ability. Starting off with faster people is likely to get you trampled, while those slower than you will hold you up. In the long run it is better to be cautious. As you become more proficient you can move up to the faster ranks.

When the gun goes off, relax. You're not Indiana Jones; don't bolt at the first sign of action. Instead, concentrate on moving easily out of the gate, maintaining control, and relaxing. The energy you save in the beginning will serve you in good stead in the final kilometers.

It's important to relax and to enjoy this new experience. If it's a marathon, make sure you drink at the feed stations and eat if you're hungry. Some contend that eating during a marathon event may be counterproductive, because some of the blood that would normally go to your arms and legs is digesting food in the stomach instead. Yet the psychological effect of knowing that Mary Davis's famous brownies are waiting for you at a feed station twenty kilometers into the Yellowstone Rendezvous can't be ignored. Don't overeat, but put something in your mouth. Be sure to thank the volunteers for their efforts (see Figure 8.3).

After you have taken your last stride and finished the race, take a second to reflect on how far you have come. You've just finished your first race, and no matter where you placed, you did a good job merely by beginning it. Bravo! Before you do anything else, change into a dry shirt, or better yet change completely into dry clothing. Your body is weak after the effort, and you must protect it against colds. After a hot drink, do some loosening-up exercises. If you feel up to it, a short, easy ski might do the trick. Don't press yourself. After your warm-down, a shower and a short nap (if you can arrange it) are in order. Marty Hall, former U.S. ski team coach, has a rule of thumb that for every hour on the racecourse you should spend an hour in bed resting.

Your nap may be shortened by travel or an awards ceremony directly at the finish of the race. Awards ceremonies are great places to meet fellow competitors and to trade information about the next race, or about waxing and training tips. It is also a great chance to give a big hand of thanks to the race organizer who spent many hours getting the race ready. There are few professional race organizers in this country; the vast majority are volunteers, as are their help. Many of them put on these races out of a love of the sport, and they deserve all the support you can give them.

Cross-country ski racing is an exciting personal adventure for everyone. With the growth of masters' skiing in this country, the popularity of marathon racing, and the development programs nationwide, we are becoming a skiing and ski racing country. A race is a chance for you to see how the elite racers ply their trade. It can also be a place where you can compete against yourself, or others of your ability.

Please see Appendix A for cross-country ski associations offering racing opportunities.

A CROSS-COUNTRY RACE CALENDAR

Following is a partial list of the bigger races in this country where you can participate in a professionally run ski competition. All the competitions listed are sanctioned by the United States Ski Association.

American Birkebeiner
P.O. Box 31
Hayward, WI 54843
715-634-2601
55k
Last weekend in February

This is the biggest cross-country ski race in the United States, with eight thousand entrants. This race has been called the citizens' Olympics, and it is thrilling to watch as well as to ski in.

California Gold Rush
P.O. Box 178
Soda Springs, CA 95728
916-426-3871
25k and 50k
Fourth weekend in March
California sunshine and spectacular
scenery; the top prize is an ounce of
gold.

Cascade Crest Marathon
P.O. Box 1031
Mt. Bachelor, OR 97709
503-382-2442
25k and 50k
Third weekend in March.
Enjoy one of Oregon's best races as
well as some of the best skiing in
the country at this time of year.

John Craig Memorial
Sisters, OR
20k
First weekend in April
This race follows the first part of
John Craig's mail route through the
pass. From the top of the pass it is a
ten-kilometer run downhill. Contact
the USSA for information.

Frisco Goldrush
P.O. Box 176
Frisco, CO 80434
15k
Second week in February
One of oldest races in this part of
the country. A perfect first-time
race with its tradition of hospitality
and capable volunteers.

Lake Placid Loppett
Mt. Van Hoevenberg X-C Area
Cascade Rd.
Lake Placid, NY 12946
518-523-2811
25k and 50k
Second weekend in January
Marathon race over the same trails
used by the Olympians in 1980.

Minnesota Finlandia
P.O. Box 771
Bemidji, MN 56601
218-751-0041
50k
First weekend in March
This event was formerly a two-day,
hundred-kilometer event but has
since been shortened. The
hospitality of Bemidji toward the
racers rivals that of many of its
European counterparts.

Presidential Ski Chase
Bretton Woods, NH 03575
603-178-5181
25k and 50k
Last weekend in January
A marathon in the shadow of the
famous Mount Washington Hotel
and Mount Washington. There's
usually good snow with an excellent
track setting at a professionally run
race.

Putney Relays
Putney School
Putney, VT 05346
802-387-5566

3x10 men's, 3x5 women's races
Second weekend in January
These relay races have been going
on for thirty years. The team events
get more exciting each year.

Red Dust Loppett
S. Front St.
Marquette, MI 49855
50k
Second week in March
The race, recently revamped, has a
new look that will bring smiles to
many faces. The face-lift has given
this race the chance to become one
of the classics.

Rosendale Ramble
Williams Hotel
Rosendale, NY 12472
212-427-1211
10k men, 5k women
First weekend in January
A season opener for folks who live
in and around New York City. A
short drive north will give you a
great race and better hospitality.

Snow Mountain Stampede
P.O. Box 36
Winter Park, CO 80282
303-726-5514
25k and 50k
Third weekend in January
A new race in a fabulous location, at
eight thousand feet in the heart of
the Rockies.

Weston Night Races
Lincoln Guide Service
Lincoln, MA 01773
617-259-9204
5–10k
Every Tuesday during the winter
Night races provide a different kind
of excitement for the spectators and
competitors. These races could fit
well into a week of training if you
live in the Boston area. A unique
feature of the Weston facility is its
ability to make snow.

Yellowstone Rendezvous
P.O. Box 65
W. Yellowstone, MT 59798
404-646-7501
25k and 50k
Second weekend in March
One of Montana's best-kept secrets
is this small, comfortable race.
(There are fewer people to crowd
the well groomed trails.) It's run
amid great scenery.

Cross-Country Ski Associations, Museums, and Organizations

Associations

Bill Koch Youth Ski League
P.O. Box 727
Brattleboro, VT 05301
802-254-6077
This is a developmental program for
cross-country and jumping aimed at
children up to thirteen years old. The
league consists of clubs all across the
United States; for a complete listing or a
club in your area, write to the address
given.

USSA Committee for
Disabled Skiers
1750 E. Boulder St.
Colorado Springs, CO 80909
Committe represents disabled skier

programs, establishes race schedules,
and recommends policy regarding
competitive skiing for people with
disabilities.

Great American Ski Chase
USSA/Olympic Complex
1750 E. Boulder St.
Colorado Springs, CO 80909
303-576-4600
This is the premier citizens' marathon
race series in the United States. Eight
races take a racer across the United States
in one winter. There are medals
presented at every race, and prizes for
completing the entire eight-race series.

The eight races are:

- Snow Mt. Stampede,
  Winter Park, CO
- Presidential Ski Chase,
  Bretton Woods, NH
- Tug Hill Tourathon,
  Lorraine, NY
- North American Vasa,
  Traverse City, MI
- American Birkebeiner,
  Hayward, WI
- Minnesota Finlandia,
  Bemidji, MN
- Yellowstone Rendezvous,
  W. Yellowstone, MT
- California Gold Rush,
  Soda Springs, CA

National Collegiate Athletic Association
  (NCAA)
P.O. Box 1906
Shawnee Mission, KS 66222
913-384-3220
This is the governing body for Divisions 1
and 2 skiing in the United States.

National Collegiate Ski Association
  (NCSA)
P.O. Box 1906
Milwaukee, WI 53213
414-257-4180
This is the governing body for the small-
college programs not associated with
Divisions 1 and 2.

Special Olympics (Winter)
c/o Walter Malmquist
1701 K St. N.W.

Washington, DC 20006
202-331-1346
The Special Olympics sponsor
international programs of physical
education, fitness, and competition for
the mentally handicapped.

United States Ski Association (USSA)
Central Division
15 Spinning Wheel Rd. No. 422
Hinsdale, IL 60521
312-325-7780
Information for the USSA programs
specific to the central area of the country
can be obtained through this office.

United States Ski Association
Eastern Division
P.O. Box 727
Brattleboro, VT 05301
802-254-6077
Write to this office for information about
the USSA programs specific to the
eastern and mid-Atlantic regions of the
country.

United States Ski Association
Western Division
Olympic Complex
1750 E. Boulder St.
Colorado Springs, CO 80909
303-578-4600
The USSA is the governing body for all
ski sport in the United States, organizing
competitions including cross-country
skiing as well as freestyle, Alpine, and
jumping contests. Write to the address
given for more information.

United States Ski Team USST/U.S.
  Educational Foundation
P.O. Box 100
Park City, UT 80909
801-649-9090
The USST is responsible for preparing
our athletes for international competition
as well as raising money to send those
athletes to competitions in this country
and overseas.

Worldloppet
CH-7504
Pontresina, Switzerland

The head office for the famous
Worldloppet marathon race series has
information about all the races.

World Wide Nordic
Rte. 8
P.O. Box 8231
Hayward WI 54843
715-634-3794
This group organizes and leads cross-
country ski trips to Europe. Trips include
all Worldloppet races and the Norwegian
huts. All trips are lead by professional
tour leaders.

United States Ski Museums

Colorado Ski Museum
c/o Pamela Horan-Kates
Vail, CO 81658
303-476-1876
The history of skiing in Colorado is
featured here.

National Ski Hall of Fame
P.O. Box 191
Ishpeming, MI 49849-0191
906-486-9281
The most complete history of skiing in
the United States is housed here, as well
as some great exhibits of skis and other
memorabilia. It's worth a stop if you are
in the area.

New England Ski Museum
Franconia, NH 03580
603-823-7177
The museum has memorabilia about the
early years of skiing in New England. A
good place to visit when the snow is a
distant memory in July.

Western American Skisport Museum
Donner Pass Memorial State Park
Truckee, CA 95734
916-587-3841
The history of western skiing is alive and
well in this museum high in the Sierra
Nevada near the famous Donner Pass.

Training Centers

Giants Ridge Training Center
P.O. Box 190
Biwabik, MN 55708
218-865-4620
A USSA-sponsored training site with
early snow and great trails for the
enthusiastic cross-country skier.

Olympic Training Center
Main Street
Lake Placid, NY 12946
518-523-2600

Olympic training center for Nordic skiing
at the site of the 1980 Winter Olympics at
Lake Placid.

Olympic Training Center
1750 E. Boulder St.
Colorado Springs, CO 80909
303-632-5551
Home of the United States Ski
Association and home of an Olympic
training and testing center.

Professional Organizations

Cross Country Ski Areas of America
P.O. Box 557
Brattleboro, VT 05301
802-257-4341
The industry representative of cross-
country ski area owners. Information
about cross-country ski centers in your
area can be obtained here.

Professional Ski Instructors of America
Plaza 7
1212 Troy Schenectady Rd.
Latham, NY 12110
518-783-1134
Certifies instructors for the cross-country
ski industry.

Ski Industries of America
8377-B Greensboro Dr.
McLean, VA 22102
703-556-9020

The industry marketing and professional
organization includes both Alpine and
Nordic representatives.

United States Ski Coaches' Association
P.O. Box 100
Park City UT 84060
801-646-9090
Certifies coaches in both Alpine and
Nordic skiing. In addition, a myriad of
information is open to all members,
including the latest innovations in
technique and training. A must for
anyone considering cross-country
coaching.

United States Ski Writers' Association
2039 S.E. 103rd Dr.
Portland, OR 97216
The professional organization of ski
writers in the United States.

Canadian Cross-Country Skiing

Canadian Ski Association
333 River Rd.
Vanier, Ont. KIL 8B9
Canada
613-741-1206
The governing body for competitive
cross-country skiing in Canada.

Canadian Ski Museum
Ottawa, Ont.
Canada
613-233-5832
The history of skiing in Canada is
wrapped up here.

Equipment Directory

Following is a listing of where you can purchase or get information on cross-country skigear, clothing, and supplies.

Akers Ski
Box 280X
Andover, ME 04216
207-392-4582
One of the oldest cross-country ski mail-order houses in the United States.

Eddie Bauer, Inc.
Fifth and Union
P.O. Box 3700
Seattle, WA 98124
800-426-8020
Mail-order your outdoor and cross-country ski clothing.

L.L. Bean
Freeport, ME 04032
207-865-4761
One of the oldest and best outdoor-product mail-order houses.

Champion Nordic Ski
Rte. 1, P.O. Box 98
Champion, MI 49814
906-339-2294
Mail-order your cross-country ski equipment.

Eagle River
P.O. Box 936N
Eagle River, WI 54521
715-479-7285
Skis to fit through the mail; a good
selection of skis.

Early Winters
110 Prefontaine Pl. S.
Seattle, WA 98104
206-624-5599
Everything and more for going out of
doors.

MSHO Sports
Putney, VT 05346
802-387-4543
Cross-country ski gear made to order.

New Moon Ski Shop
P.O. Box 132M
Hayward, WI 54843
715-634-8685
Everything for the cross-country skier,
including hard-to-get items such as roller
skis.

Nordic Sports
218 W. Bay St.
E. Tawas, MI 48730
517-362-2001
Another mail-order house; send for the
catalog to compare prices.

Odlo USA
69 N. Main St.
Farmington, ME 04938
207-778-9508

Fashionable and innovative cross-country
ski clothing.

Ole's Innovative Sports
6967 Washington Ave.
S. Minneapolis, MN 55435
612-944-6726
The place to purchase the marathon
skate.

Reliable Racing Supply, Inc.
624 Glen St.
Glens Falls, NY 12801
518-793-5677
A complete cross-country ski shop: event
supplies and off-season training supplies.

REI
P.O. Box C88125
Seattle, WA 98188
800-426-4840
Another famous mail-order house for
great outdoor equipment.

Scandinavian Ski Shop
40 W. 57th St.
New York, NY 10019
212-757-8524
Cross-country gear in the heart of New
York City.

Sunbuster
15115 N.E. 90th St.
Redmond, WA 98052
206-883-6646
Skiwear and skiwear accessories.

Trek and Trail
Hwy U.S. 2
Bessemer, MI 49911
906-663-4791
Mail order cross-country ski equipment
with a 20% discount for USSA members.

Turner Competition Services
P.O. Box 3131
Park City, UT 84060

801-649-5063
Event supplier specializing in ski racing
(bibs, banner, etc.).

V.O. Max
Dept. E, P.O. Box 21
Plainfield, MA 01070
617-444-7587
Cross-country ski clothing made to order.

Following is a partial listing of places to purchase training devices.

Exer-Genie

Reliable Racing Supply, Inc.
624 Glen St.
Glens Falls, NY 12801

Indoor Cross-Country Simulators

Fitness Master, Inc.
Chanhassen Lakes Business Center
1387 Park Rd.
Chanhassen, MN 55317

Nordic Track
124 Columbia Ct.
Chaska, MN 55318

Roller Skates

Ole's Innovative Sports
6967 Washington Ave.
Minneapolis, MN 55435

Roller Skis

Edsbyn Sport, Inc.
860 Decatur Ave. N.
Minneapolis, MN 55441

Rolleto
Sepp Sport, Inc.
1805 Monroe St.
Madison, WI 53711

SweNor
Reliable Racing Supply, Inc.
624 Glen St.
Glens Falls, NY 12801

Swede Ski
The Swede Sports, Inc.
7200 Ohms Ln.
Minneapolis, MN 55435

The following manufacturers sell racing, touring, and telemark boots and bindings in this country. For further information on the boots and bindings and where to purchase them, call or write to the address given.

Adidas
3011 N. First St.
San Jose, CA 95134
408-946-4333

Alpina
Alpina Sports Corp.
P.O. Box 23
Hanover, NH 03755
603-448-3101

Asolo
Kenko International, Inc.
8141 W I-70 Frontage Rd.
Arvada, CO 80002
303-425-1200

DMC Technical
Avant 1
Diemolding Corporation
Canastota, NY 13032
315-697-2221

Dovre
P.O. Box 339
Shelburne, VT 05482
802-985-8044

Dynafit
Fischer of America, Inc.
35 Industrial Pkwy.
Woburn, MA 01801
617-935-2452

Edsbyn
Edsbyn Sport, Inc.
860 Decatur Ave. N.
Minneapolis, MN 55427
612-546-1343

Geze
Elan-Monark
208 Flynn Ave.
S. Burlington, VT 05401
802-863-5593

Jalas
Jarvinen USA
47 Congress St.
Salem, MA 01970
617-744-8037

Karhu
Karhu-Titan USA, Inc.
55 Green Mountain Dr.
Burlington, VT 05401
802-864-4519

Marker
Marker USA
P.O. Box 1526
Salt Lake City, UT 84110
801-584-6262

Norboot
Norski of America Ltd.
1642 Doty St.
Oshkosh, WI 54901
414-233-6409

Nortur, Inc.
2000 E. Center Cir.
Minneapolis, MN 55441
612-559-1500

Salomon
Salomon/North America
4000 Salomon Cir.
Sparks, NV 89431
800-648-4880

Skiing Finn
Exel, Inc.
10-D Roessler Rd.
Woburn, MA 01801
617-933-0217

Suveren
Volvo of America
Recreational Products Div.
Bldg. G

Rockleigh, NJ 07647
201-768-7300

Swix
Swix Sport USA
Tracy Rd.
Chelmsford, MA 01824
617-256-6595

Trak
Trak, Inc.
P.O. Box 178
187 Neck Pond
Ward Hill, MA 01830
617-374-0713

Tyrol
Tyrol USA
50 Jonergin Dr.
Swanton, VT 05488
802-868-7331

The following manufacturers sell racing and touring poles in the United States.

Dovre
Dovre Ski Products
P.O. Box 339
Shelburne, VT 05482
802-985-8044

Exel
Exel, Inc.
10-D Roessler Rd.
Woburn, MA 01801
617-933-0217

Fuji
Fuji America
1840 Northwestern Ave.
Garnee, IL 60031
312-336-0450

Jarvinen
Jarvinen USA
47 Congress St.
P.O. Box 46
Salem, MA 01970
617-744-8037

Karhu
Karhu-Titan USA, Inc.
55 Green Mountain Dr.
Burlington, VT 05401
802-864-4519

Life Link
Life Link International
P.O. Box 2913
1240 Huff Ln.
Jackson, WY 83001
800-443-8620

Moon
Edsbyn Sport, Inc.
800 Decatur Ave. N.
Minneapolis, MN 55427
612-546-1313

Sixtens
Reliable Racing Supply
624 Glen St.

Glens Falls, NY 12081
518-793-5677

Swix
Swix Sport USA
Tracy Rd.
Chelmsford, MA 01824
617-256-6595

Tomic
Tomic Golf and Ski Mfg., Inc.
23102 Mariposa Ave.
Torrance, CA 90502
213-534-2532

Trak
Trak, Inc.
P.O. Box 178
187 Neck Rd.
Ward Hill, MA 01830
617-374-0713

Following is a partial listing of manufacturers who sell racing, touring, and telemark skis in this country. For further information on the skis, write to the address given.

Adidas
Libco/Adidas
One Silver Ct.
Springfield, NJ 07081
201-379-1630

Asnes
Bauer Cycle Supply
404 Third Ave. N.
Minneapolis, MN 55401
612-333-2581

Atomic
Atomic Ski USA, Inc.
4 Cote Ln.
Bedford, NH 03102
603-668-8980

Dynastar
Dynastar Skis, Inc.
P.O. Box 25, Hercules Dr.
Colchester, VT 05446
802-655-2400

Edsbyn
Edsbyn Sport, Inc.
860 Decatur Ave. N.
Minneapolis, MN 55427
612-546-1343

Elan
Elan-Monarck
208 Flynn Ave.
S. Burlington, VT 05401
802-863-5593

Epoke
Nortur
2060 E. Center Cir.
Minneapolis, MN 55441
612-559-1500

Fischer
Fischer of America, Inc.
35 Industrial Pkwy.
Woburn, MA 01801

Fuji
Fuji of America
1840 Northwestern Ave.
Garnee, IL 60031
312-336-0450

Jarvinen
Jarvinen USA
47 Congress St.
P.O. Box 46
Salem, MA 01970
617-744-8037

Karhu
Karhu-Titan USA, Inc.

55 Green Mountain Dr.
Burlington, VT 05401
802-864-4519

Kastle
Kastle USA, Inc.
P.O. Box 1208
Bldg. E-16
Freeport Center
Clearfield, VT 84016
801-776-6060

Kneissl
Kneissl, Inc.
P.O. Box 178
187 Neck Rd.
Ward Hill, MA 01830
617-374-0713

Norski
Norski of America
1642 Doty St.
Oshkosh, WI 54901
414-233-6409

Rossignol
Rossignol Ski Co., Inc.
Industrial Ave.
P.O. Box 298
Williston, VT 05495
802-863-2511

Skilom
Volvo of America Corporation
Recreational Products Div.
Bldg. G
Rockleigh, NJ 07647
201-768-7300

Splitkein
c/o F.H. Weissner
159 Lakeside Ave.
P.O. Box 523
Burlington, VT 05401
802-863-3484

Sundins
Reliable Racing Supply
624 Glen St.
Glens Falls, NY 12801
518-793-5677

Trak
Trak, Inc.
P.O. Box 178
187 Neck Rd.
Ward Hill, MA 01830
617-374-0713

Volkl
Volkl USA, Inc.
P.O. Box 206
Banner Elk, NC 28604
704-898-4536

Cross-Country Ski Clubs

Clubs in this country range from the social to the highly competitive, from highly organized to loosely structured. The benefit of belonging to a cross-country ski club is that the members share the same interests as you do. Contact the club nearest you and see what their specific interests are. Some ski clubs are highly organized and can fill every need, others may simply be clubs for the fun of it.

Phone numbers for many of the clubs are unavailable because they change every year, as do the presidents or secretaries of the club.

Alaska

Nordic Ski Club of Anchorage
P.O. Box 3301
Anchorage, AK 99501

Nordic Ski Club of Fairbanks
P.O. Box 80111
Fairbanks, AK 99708
907-479-2719

Salcha Ski Club
P.O. Box 140055
Salcha, AK 99714
907-488-6684

California

Auburn Ski Club
c/o Lew Fellows
8465 Barton Rd.
Roseville, CA 95678

Olympic Valley School
P.O. Box 2353
Olympic Valley, CA 95730
916-583-1558

Westwood SC
P.O. Box 24534
Los Angeles, CA 90024

Colorado

Colorado High School Ski Team
c/o Richard Bryant
Clear Creek Secondary P.O. Box 3369
Idaho Springs, CO 80452

Lake Eldora Racing Team
LE5815 Rustic Knolls
Boulder, CO 80301
303-447-8014

Steamboat Springs Winter Sports
P.O. Box 285
Steamboat Springs, CO 80477

Winter Park SC
P.O. Box 36
Winter Park, CO 80482
303-726-5514

Idaho

Bogus Basin Ski Racing Alliance
2405 Bogus Basin Rd.

Boise, ID 83702
208-343-1891

Illinois

Four Winds Ski Club
P.O. Box 577
Hoffman Estates, IL 60195

Norge Ski Club
100 Ski Hill Rd.
Fox River Grove, IL 60021

Maine

Down East Ski Club
70 Forest Ave.
Portland, ME 04103
207-773-1736

Massachusetts

Eaglebrook Ski Club
c/o Jack Shea
Deerfield, MA 01342
413-774-7411

Williams Outing Club
S.U. Box 3304
Williams College
Williamstown, MA 01267
413-597-2317

Michigan

Fremont Ski Club
P.O. Box 144
Fremont, MI 49412
616-924-2626

GM Ski Club
894 Englewood
Rochester, MI 48063
313-375-0334

Metro Detroit Ski Council
President
P.O. Box 605
Dearborn, MI 48121

Minnesota

Minneapolis Ski Club
c/o Ronald Carlson
9315 S. Cedar Lake Rd.
St. Louis Park, MN 55426
612-545-2995

St. Paul S.C.
c/o Tom Harrington
2278 Timberlea Dr.
Woodbury, MN 55125
612-735-2765

Montana

Glacier Nordic Club
c/o Doug Pitman, M.D.
1 Tideway
Whitefish, MT 59937
406-862-3858

Nevada

Reno Ski & Recreation Club
1555 Ridgeview Dr. 3236
Reno, NV 89509
702-827-6919

New Hampshire

Crotched Mtn. Ski Club
Mtn. Rd.
Francestown, NH 03043
603-588-6345

Dartmouth Outing Club
Box 9
Hanover, NH 03755

Holderness School SC
c/o Dennis Donahue
Holderness School
Plymouth, NH 03264
603-536-1257

Massa Schussers Ski Club
P.O. Box 25
Glen, NH 03838
603-383-6372

Mt. Sunapee Area Ski Club
P.O. Box 221
Mt. Sunapee, NH 03772

Nansen Ski Club
c/o Leon Costello
Berlin, NH 03570

New England College Ski Team
P.O. Box 76
New England College
Henniker, NH 03242
603-428-2263

Ski Wheelers SC
P.O. Box 17
Kearsarge, NH 03847
603-356-9793

Waterville Valley BBTS
Waterville Valley, NH 03223
603-236-8601

New Jersey

Telemark Ski Club
362 Sussex Ave.
Morristown, NJ 07960
201-267-6879

New Mexico

Taos Sports Associates
P.O. Box 69
Taos Ski Valley, NM 87571
505-776-2437

New York

Holiday Valley Jr. Racing Camp
P.O. Box A
Ellicottville, NY 14731
716-699-2345

Irondequoit Club
Piseco, NY 12139

Lake Placid Ski Club
Lake Placid, NY 12946

Lapland Lake Nordic Ski Club
RD 2 Benson
Northville, NY 12134

New York State SR Nordic
21 Roberts Ln.
Saratoga Springs, NY 12866
518-584-2256

Polar Bear Ski Club
c/o Beatrice Foley
P.O. Box 625
Old Forge, NY 13420
315-369-3683

Rosendale Nordic Ski Club
Rosendale, New York 12472

Oregon

Cooper Spur Race Team
2884 Paasch Dr.
Hood River, OR 97031
503-386-4234

Meadows Amateur Ski Racing Association
19161 Pacific Highway
West Linn, OR 97068
503-635-6566

Ski Trek Ski Club
P.O. Box 500
Beaverton, OR 97077
503-646-1601

Vermont

Bromley Outing Club
P.O. Box 17
Peru, VT 05152
802-362-1987

Burke Mtn. Academy
P.O. Box 78

East Burke, VT 05832
802-626-5607

Comey's Comets
P.O. Box 1169
Stowe, VT 05672
802-253-8467

Lyndon Outing SC
Lyndon State College
Lyndonville, VT 05851
802-626-9371

Putney Ski Club
Putney School
West Hill
Putney, VT 05346

Stratton Mtn. Ski Club
Stratton Mtn. School
Stratton Mtn., VT 05155
802-297-2325

Vermont Academy SC
Vermont Academy
Saxtons River, VT 05451
802-869-2121

Woodstock Ski Runners
P.O. Box 2
S. Pomfret, VT 05067
802-457-3426

Washington

Boeing Ski Club "Ski Bacs"
16018 46th Ave. S.
Seattle, WA 98188
206-248-2421

Inland Empire Nordic Club
P.O. Box 1729
Spokane, WA 99203
509-535-2617

Kongsberger Ski Club
106 232nd Pl. S.W.
Bothell, WA 98021
206-483-0978

Leavenworth Winter Sports Club
c/o Clarence Ostella
224 Orchard St.
Leavenworth, WA 98826

Team Ski Acres
5524 25th Ave. N.E.
Seattle, WA 98105
206-527-2082

The Yahoos
2302 N.W. Blue Ridge Dr.
Seattle, WA 98177
206-782-7317

Wisconsin

Nordic SC of Milwaukee, Inc.
c/o Gary Hansen
10163 W. Forest Home Ave. No. 206
Hales Corners, WI 53130
414-425-8602

Tri-Norse SC
c/o Ronald Larson
1240 Franklin St.
Wisconsin Rapids, WI 54494
715-423-8905

Where to Ski: A Nationwide Listing of the Top Spots

Following is a partial list of the cross-country ski areas in the United States. In certain cases not all the information is available; be sure to call the area in advance. The list is subject to change because some areas may close and others open. Before you head out to go skiing, be sure to contact the area to see if they are operating. In many cases there will be a charge to ski on the trails.

1. Groomed trails
2. Rentals
3. Instruction
4. Events

5. Lodging
6. Meals
7. Trail fees

Glacier National Park. (UNITED STATES SKI ASSOCIATION)

Alaska

Alyeska Resort
P.O. Box 249
Girdwood, AK 99587
907-783-2222
1, 2, 3, 5, 6

Birch Hill Ski Area
Fairbanks Chamber of Commerce
Fairbanks, AK 99701
907-586-5284

Eaglecrest Ski Area
115 S. Seward
Juneau, AK 99801
907-586-5284

Hatcher Pass Ski Touring
P.O. Box 2655
Palmer, AK 99645
907-745-5897
1, 2, 3, 4, 5, 6, 7

Nordic Ski Club of Anchorage
P.O. Box 3301
Anchorage, AK 99501
907-277-0827

Prism Ski Touring
P.O. Box 136
Girdwood, AK 99587
907-783-2945
1, 2, 3, 4, 5, 6

Arizona

Alpine Country Club
P.O. Box 349
Alpine, AZ 85920
602-339-4944

Circle B Market
P.O. Box 121
Greer, AZ 85927
602-735-7540
1, 2, 3, 4, 5, 6

Greer Ski Tours
P.O. Box 190
Greer, AZ 85927
602-735-7555

Montezuma Nordic Center
P.O. Box 497
Mormon Lake, AZ 86038
602-354-2220
1, 2, 3, 4, 5, 6, 7

Mormon Lake Ski Touring Center
P.O. Box 18
Mormon Lake, AZ 86038
602-354-2240
1, 2, 3, 4, 5, 6, 7

Sacred Mountain Tours
317 N. Humphreys St.
Flagstaff, AZ 86001
602-774-7809
1, 2, 3, 4, 5, 6

Wild and Scenic, Inc.
P.O. Box 460
Flagstaff, AZ 86002
602-774-7343
2, 3, 4, 5, 6, 7

California

Alpine Adventures
P.O. Box 283
Markleeville, CA 96120
919-694-2466
3, 4, 5, 7

Aschi Sport Cross Country
P.O. Box 16549
S. Lake Tahoe, CA 95706
916-544-7873

Bear Lake Valley Nordic
P.O. Box 5
Bear Valley, CA 95223
209-753-2844
1, 2, 3, 4, 5, 6, 7

Bear Valley Nordic Center
P.O. Box 5207
Bear Valley, CA 95223
209-753-2834

Big Chief Cross-Country
P.O. Box 2477
Olympic Valley, CA 95730
916-587-4723

Buffalo Bill's
40286 Big Bear Blvd.
Big Bear Lake, CA 92315
714-866-5253

Castle Lake Nordic Center
P.O. Box 660
Mt. Shasta, CA 96067
916-926-5555
1, 2, 3, 4, 5, 6, 7

Eagle Mt. Nordic
P.O. Box 89
Emigrant Gap, CA 95715
916-389-2254
1, 2, 3, 4, 5, 6, 7

Ebbetts Pass STC
Tamarack Lodge
P.O. Box 657
Bear Valley, CA 95223
209-753-2080

Echo Summit Nordic Center
P.O. Box 8955
South Lake Tahoe, CA 95364
916-659-7154
1, 2, 3, 4, 6, 7

Fifth Season
426 N. Mt. Shasta Blvd.
P.O. Box 117
Mt. Shasta, CA 96067
916-926-2776

Frazier Ski & Pack STC
P.O. Box 660, Star Route
Frazier Park, CA 93225
805-245-3438

Grant Grove Ski Touring
King's Canyon National Park, CA 93633
209-335-2314

Kirkwood Cross-Country
P.O. Box 77
Kirkwood, CA 95646
209-258-8864
1, 2, 3, 4, 5, 6, 7

Lassen Ski Touring
2150 Main St.
Suite 7
Red Bluff, CA 96080
916-529-1512
2, 3, 4, 5, 6

Leland Meadow Nordic Center
P.O. Box 1498
Pinecrest, CA 95364
209-965-3745
1, 2, 3, 5, 6, 7

Little Norway Resort
P.O. Little Norway
Little Norway, CA 95721
916-659-7181
1, 2, 3, 5, 6

Mammoth Cross-Country Ski Area
P.O. Box 69
Mammoth Lakes, CA 93546
619-934-2442

Montecito-Sequoia
1485 Redwood Dr.
Los Altos, CA 94022
415-967-8612
1, 2, 3, 5, 6

Northstar Nordic Center
P.O. Box 129
Truckee, CA 95734
916-562-1113
1, 2, 3, 4, 5, 6, 7

Quiet Mountain Nordic
P.O. Box 1010
Nevada City, CA 95959

916-265-9186
1, 2, 5, 6

Rock Creek Winter Lodge
Rte. 1, P.O. Box 5
Mammoth Lakes, CA 93546
619-935-4464
1, 2, 3, 5, 6

Royal Gorge X-C Ski Resort
P.O. Box 178
Soda Springs, CA 95728
916-426-3871
1, 2, 3, 4, 5, 6, 7

Sequoia Ski Touring
Sequoia & Kings National Park
Sequoia, CA 93262
209-565-3308
1, 2, 3, 4, 5, 6

Sierra Meadows STC
P.O. Box D4
Mammoth Lakes, CA 93546
619-935-4606
1, 2, 5, 6

Snow Summit Nordic Center
P.O. Box 77
Big Bear Lake, CA 92315
714-866-6117

Squaw Valley
P.O. Box 2637
Olympic Valley, CA 95730
916-583-4211

Strawberry Lodge XC Ski Center
Hwy. 50
Kyburz, CA 95720
916-659-7200
1, 2, 3, 4, 5, 6

Tahoe Donner Touring Center
P.O. Box 2462
Truckee, CA 95734
916-587-9821
1, 2, 3, 4, 5, 6, 7

Tahoe Nordic Ski Center
P.O. Box 1632
Tahoe City, CA 95730
916-583-9858
1, 2, 3, 4, 6

Tamarack Ski Touring Center
Tamarack
P.O. Box 5067
Bear Valley, CA 95223
209-753-2594
1, 2, 3, 5, 6, 7

Telemark Country Sports
P.O. Box 11975
Tahoe Paradise, CA 95708
916-577-6811
1, 2, 3, 5, 6, 7

Yosemite Mountaineering School
Yosemite National Park, CA 95389
209-372-1244
1, 2, 3, 4, 5, 6

Colorado

Alfred Braun Hut System
702 W. Main St.

Aspen, CO 81611
303-349-5408

Ambush Ski Touring Center
P.O. Box 1230
Crested Butte, CO 91224
303-349-5408
1, 2, 3, 5, 6, 7

Ashcroft Ski Touring
P.O. Box 1572
Aspen, CO 81611
303-925-1971
1, 2, 3, 5, 6, 7

Bear Pole Ranch
Star Rte. 1
Steamboat Springs, CO 80477
303-247-0111
1, 2, 3, 4, 5, 6, 7

Bear Ranch
Hwy. 550
Durango, CO 81301
303-453-6617
1, 2, 3, 4, 5, 6, 7

Breckenridge Nordic Ski Center
P.O. Box 1058
Breckenridge, CO 80446
303-453-6617
1, 2, 3, 4, 5, 6, 7

C Lazy U Ranch
P.O. Box 378
Granby, CO 80446
303-887-3344
1, 2, 3, 5, 6, 7

Colorado Outward Bound School
945 Pennsylvania St.
Denver, CO 80203
303-837-0880
1, 2, 3, 5, 6, 7

Copper Mountain Touring Center
P.O. Box 1
Copper Mountain, CO 80443
303-968-2882
1, 2, 3, 4, 5, 6, 7

Crooked Creek Ski Touring
P.O. Box 3142
Vail, CO 81658
303-949-5682
1, 2, 3, 4, 5, 6, 7

Cuchara Valley Cross-Country Center
P.O. Box 459
La Veta, CO 81055
303-258-3211
1, 2, 3, 5, 6

Devil's Thumb Ranch
P.O. Box 8188
Winter Park, CO 80482
303-726-9446
1, 2, 3, 4, 5, 6, 7

Eldora Touring Center
P.O. Box 430
Nederland, CO 80466
303-258-3211
1, 2, 3, 4, 5, 6, 7

Frisco, Town of
P.O. Box 370

Frisco, CO 80443
303-668-5276

Glen Eden Ranch
P.O. Box 867
Clark, CO 80428
303-879-3906
1, 2, 3, 4, 5, 6, 7

Keystone Ski Resort
P.O. Box 38
Keystone, CO 80446
303-468-2316

Nordic Adventure Ski Tour Center
P.O. Box 528
Crested Butte, CO 81224
303-349-2250
1, 2, 3, 4, 5, 6

Pagosa Pines Touring Center
P.O. Box 119
Pagosa Springs, CO 81147
303-264-2403
1, 2, 3, 4, 5, 6

Peaceful Valley Ski Ranch
Star Rd.
Lyons, CO 80540
303-264-2403
1, 2, 3, 5, 6

Redstone Inn STC
82 Redstone Blvd.
Redstone, CO 81623
303-963-2526

Rocky Mt. Ski Tours
P.O. Box 413
Estes Park, CO 80517
303-586-2114
2, 3, 5, 6

Scandinavian Lodge
P.O. Box 5040
Steamboat Village, CO 80499
303-879-0517
1, 2, 3, 4, 5, 6, 7

Snowmass Ski Touring Center
Aspen Ski Corporation
Aspen, CO 81611
303-925-1220
1, 2, 3, 4, 5, 7

Snow Mountain Ranch
P.O. Box 558
Granby, CO 80446
303-887-2152
1, 2, 3, 4, 5, 6, 7

Steamboat Ski Touring
P.O. Box 5040
Steamboat Village, CO 80499
303-879-6111
1, 2, 3, 4, 5, 6, 7

Sunlight Ski Touring Center
c/o Chilton's Sporting Goods
208 Sixth St.
Glenwood Springs, CO 81601
303-945-7380
1, 2, 3, 4, 5, 6, 7

Tamarron
P.O. Drawer 3131

Durango, CO 81301
303-247-8801
1, 2, 3, 5, 6

Telluride Ski Touring
P.O. Box 672
Ophir, CO 81426
303-728-3856
1, 2, 3, 4, 5, 6, 7

Tour Idlewild
P.O. Box 1
Hideway Park, CO 80450
303-726-5564
1, 2, 3, 4, 5, 6, 7

USSA The Alfred Braun Hut System
702 W. Main St.
Aspen, CO 81611
303-925-7162

Vail/Beaver Creek Cross-Country Ski
  Center
458 Vail Valley Dr.
Vail, CO 81657
303-476-3239
1, 2, 3, 4, 5, 6, 7

Vista Verde Guest Ranch
P.O. Box 465
Steamboat Springs, CO 80477
303-879-3858
1, 2, 3, 5, 6

West Peak Mountaineering
P.O. Box 459
La Veta, CO 81055
303-742-3661

Connecticut

Blackberry River
Main St.
Norfolk, CT 06050
203-542-5100

Cedar Brooks Farms STC
1481 Ratley Rd.
West Suffield, CT 06093
203-668-5026
1, 2, 3, 4, 5, 6, 7

Pine Mt. STC
Rte. 179
E. Hartland, CT 06027
203-653-4279

Powder Ridge
99 Powder Hill Rd.
Middlefield, CT 06455
203-886-2284
1, 2, 3, 4, 5, 6, 7

Quinebaug Valley
R.F.D. 3, P.O. Box 23
Norwich, CT 06360
203-886-2284
1, 2, 3, 5, 6, 7

Riverrunning and Ski Touring
  Expeditions
Main St.
Falls Village, CT 06031
203-824-5579
1, 2, 3, 5, 6, 7

Winding Trails Ski Touring Center
1150 Farmington Ave.
Rte. 4

Farmington, CT 06032
203-678-9582
1, 2, 3, 4, 5, 6, 7

Woodbury Ski and Racquet
Rte. 47
Woodbury, CT 06798
203-263-2203
1, 2, 3, 4, 5, 6, 7

Idaho

Alpenrose Hotel/Galena Touring Center
P.O. Box 1066
Sun Valley, ID 83353
208-726-4010
1, 2, 3, 4, 6, 7

Busterback Ranch
Star Rte.
Ketchum, ID 83340
208-774-2217
1, 2, 3, 4, 5, 6, 7

Elkhorn at Sun Valley
P.O. Box 1067
Sun Valley, ID 83353
208-622-4511

Sun Valley Nordic Center
P.O. Box 272
Sun Valley, ID 83353
208-622-4111
1, 2, 3, 4, 5, 6, 7

Teton Mountain Touring
P.O. Box 514
Driggs, ID 83422
208-354-2768
1, 2, 3, 4, 5, 6

Wilderness River Outfitters
P.O. Box 871
Salmon, ID 83467
208-756-3959
1, 2, 3, 4, 5, 6

Wood River Nordic
P.O. Box 3637
Ketchum, ID 83340
208-726-3266

Illinois

Eagle Ridge Nordic Ski Center
P.O. Box 777
Galena, IL 61036
815-777-2500
1, 2, 3, 5, 6, 7

Norge STC
100 Ski Hill Rd.
Fox River Grove, IL 60021
312-639-9718

Sportsman's Golf Course
3535 Dundee Rd.
Northbrook, IL 60062
312-291-2350

Indiana

Gnaw Bone Camp Cross-
    Country Ski Area
R.R. 2, P.O. Box 91
Nashville, IN 47448
812-988-4852
1, 2, 3, 5, 6, 7

Maine

Akers Ski
Andover, ME 04216
207-392-4582
1, 2, 3, 4, 5, 6, 7

The Bethel Inn
Broad St.
Bethel, ME 04217
207-824-2175
1, 2, 3, 5, 6, 7

The Birches on Moosehead Lake
Rockwood, ME 04478
207-824-2175
1, 2, 3, 4, 5, 6, 7

Little Lyford Pond Lodge
P.O. Box 688
Brownville, ME 04970
207-695-2821
1, 2, 3, 5, 6

Ski Nordic at Saddleback
P.O. Box 671
Rangley, ME 04970
207-658-9200

Summit Springs, STC
P.O. Box 455
Poland Springs, ME 04274
207-998-4515

Sunday River Ski Touring
R.F.D. 2, P.O. Box 141
Bethel, ME 04217
207-824-2410
1, 2, 3, 4, 5, 6, 7

Massachusetts

Brodie Mountain Ski Touring Center
Rte. 7
New Ashford, MA 01237
413-443-4752
1, 2, 3, 4, 5, 6, 7

Bucksteep Manor Ski Touring Center
Washington Mt., MA 01223
413-623-5535
1, 2, 3, 4, 5, 6, 7

Butternut Ski Touring
Butternut Basin, Rte. 23
Great Barrington, MA 01230
413-528-2000
1, 2, 3, 6

Cummington Farms STC
South Rd.
Cummington, MA 01026
413-634-2111
1, 2, 3, 4, 5, 6, 7

The Egremont Inn STC
S. Egremont, MA 01258
413-528-2111

Gordon College STC
34 Hull St.
Beverly, MA 01915
617-927-2300

Great Brook Farms STC
Lowell St.
Carlisle, MA 01741

Hickory Hill Touring Center
P.O. Box 39
Worthington, MA 01098
413-238-5813
1, 2, 3, 5, 6, 7

Jug End Resort
S. Egremont, MA 01258
413-528-0434
1, 2, 5, 6, 7

Lincoln Guide Service
Lincoln Rd.
P.O. Box 100
Lincoln, MA 01773
617-259-9204
1, 2, 3, 4, 5, 6, 7

Northfield Mountain STC
RR 1, P.O. Box 377
Northfield, MA 01360
413-659-3714
1, 2, 3, 5, 6, 7

Oak Ridge STC
W. Gill Rd.
Gill, MA 01327
413-863-9693

Otis Ridge Ski Area
Rte. 23
Otis Ridge, MA 01253
413-269-4444
1, 2, 3, 5, 6, 7

Peaceful Acres STC
Hubbardston, MA 01452
617-928-4413

Roadsend Trails
P.O. Box 62
North Egremont, MA 01250
413-528-3172
1, 2, 3, 5, 6, 7

Rolling Green Ski Touring
311 Lowell St.
Andover, MA 01339
617-475-4066

Shaker Farms
Shaker Road
Westfield, MA 01085
413-562-2770
1, 2, 3, 4, 5, 6, 7

Stump Sprouts
West Hill Rd.
Charlement, MA 01339
413-339-4265
1, 2, 3, 5, 6, 7

The Warren Center
529 Chestnut St.
Ashland, MA 01721
617-881-1142

Waschusett Mountain Ski Area
Mountain Rd.
Princeton, MA 01541
617-464-2355
1, 2, 3, 4, 5, 6, 7

Waubeeka STC
Rte. 7
Williamstown, MA 01267
413-458-5869

YMCA Outdoor Center
East St.
Hopkinton, MA 01748
617-435-9345
1, 2, 3, 4, 5, 6, 7

Michigan

Alpine Valley Ski Area
6775 & Highland Rd.
Milford, MI 48042
313-887-2180

Boyne Nordican
Boyne Falls, MI 49713
616-549-2441
1, 2, 3, 4, 5, 6, 7

Champion Nordic Ski Area
Nor M-95
Champion, MI 49814
906-339-2294

Cool XC Touring Center
5337 210th Ave.
LeRoy, MI 49655
616-768-4624
1, 2, 3, 4, 5, 6, 7

Corsair Ski Trails
Monument Rd.
East Tawas, MI 48730
517-362-2001
1, 2, 4, 5, 6

Dunham Hills Golf Club
P.O. Box 602
Bloomfield, MI 48042
313-887-9170

Farmington Hills Park
31555 Eleven Hills Rd.
Farmington Hills, MI 48018
313-474-6115

Hanson Recreation Area
P.O. Box 361
Grayling, MI 49738
517-348-9266
1, 2, 3, 4, 5, 6, 7

Heavner XC Ski Area (Milford)
2775 Garden Rd.
Milford, MI 48042
313-685-2379
2, 3, 5, 6

Heavner XC Ski Area (Proudlake)
2775 Garden Rd.
Milford, MI 48042
313-685-2379
1, 2, 3, 5, 6

Hilton Shanty Creek
P.O. Box 255
Bellaire, MI 49615
616-533-8626
1, 2, 3, 4, 5, 6, 7

Hinchman Acres Resort and
X-C Skiing Center
702 N. Morenci
Mio, MI 48647
517-826-3991
1, 2, 3, 5, 6, 7

Independence Oaks Park
9501 Sashalsow Rd.

Clarkston, MI 48016
313-625-0877
1, 2, 3, 4, 5, 6, 7

Love County Creek Park
233L Huckleberry Ln.
Berrien Center, MI 49935
616-471-2617
1, 2, 3, 4, 5, 6, 7

Schuss MTN-Karhu STC
Schuss Mountain
Mancelona, MI 49659
616-471-2617
1, 2, 3, 4, 5, 6, 7

Ski Brute
P.O. Box 165
Iron River, MI 49935
906-265-4957
1, 2, 3, 5, 6, 7

Sugar Loaf Mountain Resort
Rte. 1
Cedar, MI 49621
616-228-5461
1, 2, 3, 5, 6, 7

Suicide Bowl
201 E. Division St.
Ishpeming, MI 49849

Timberlane Nordic Ski Center
Irons, MI 49644
616-266-5780
1, 2, 3, 4, 5, 6, 7

Troy Park and Recreation
5725 Rochester Rd.
Troy, MI 48084
313-624-3484

Tur-Ski-Ree
7801 N. 46th St.
Augusta, MI 49012
616-731-5266

Windmill Ski Touring Center
Boyne City Rd.
Charlevoix, MI 49720
616-547-2746
1, 2, 3, 4, 5, 6, 7

Minnesota

Bearskin Lodge Ski Touring Center
P.O. Box 10, Gunflint Trail
Grand Marais, MN 55604
218-388-2292
1, 2, 3, 4, 5, 6

Blueberry Hills
P.O. Box 363A
Deer River, MN 56636
218-246-8010

Borderland Lodge
P.O. Box 102, Gunflint Trail
Grand Marais, MN 55604
218-388-2233
1, 3, 5, 6

Boundary Country Trekking
Gunflint Trl. 67-1
Grand Marais, MN 55604
218-388-4487
1, 2, 3, 4, 5, 6, 7

Buena Vista Ski Area
P.O. Box 308
Bemidji, MN 56601
218-751-5530
1, 2, 3, 4, 5, 6

Cascade Lodge
Lutsen, MN 55612
218-387-1112

Cedar Springs Lodge
Cass County Courthouse
Walker, MN 56484
218-836-2248

Duluth Parks and Recreation
Room 208, City Hall
Duluth, MN 55802
218-723-3337

Eagle Mountain Ski and Camping Area
Gray Eagle, MN 56336
612-285-4567
1, 2, 4, 5, 6, 7

Grand Portage Lodge
P.O. Box 307
Grand Portage, MN 55605
218-475-2401
1, 2, 5, 6

Gunflint Trl.
Box 100 Gunflint Trl.
Grand Marais, MN 55604
218-338-2294
1, 2, 3, 5, 6

Minnesota Zoo
12101 Johnny Cake Rd.

Apple Valley, MN 55124
218-432-9000

National Forest Lodge
3226 Hwy. 1
Isabella, MN 55607
218-323-7676
1, 2, 3, 4, 5, 6

Norwester Lodge
P.O. Box 60
Grand Marais, MN 55604
218-388-2252
1, 5, 6

Quanda Mountain Touring Center
Hill, MN 55748
218-697-2324
1, 2, 3, 4, 5, 6, 7

Spider Lake Ski Touring
P.O. Box 34
Backus, MN 56435
218-326-8286

Spidhal Ski Gard
Erhard, MN 56534
218-736-5097
1, 2, 3, 4, 5, 6, 7

Spirit Mountain
Duluth, MN 55810
218-628-2891
1, 2, 3, 4, 5, 6, 7

Sugar Hills/Sugar Lodge
P.O. Box 369
Grand Rapids, MN 55744

218-326-0535
1, 2, 3, 4, 5, 6, 7

Theodore Wirth Ski Area
Plymouth and Wirth Pkwy.
Minneapolis, MN 55422
612-522-4584
1, 2, 3, 4, 5, 6, 7

Val Chatel
Park Rapids, MN 56470
218-266-3306
1, 2, 5, 6, 7

Windigo Lodge
G.T. Box 67
Grand Marais, MN 55604
218-388-2222
1, 5, 6

Montana

Chico Hot Springs
Pray, MT 59065
406-333-4411
1, 2, 3, 5, 6

Crosscut Ranch
Bozeman, MT 59715
406-587-3122
1, 2, 3, 4, 5, 6, 7

Desert Mountain Ranch
P.O. Box 157
West Glacier, MT 59936
406-387-5248

Elkhorn Hot Springs
P.O. Box 514
Polaris, MT 59746
406-834-3434

Fairmont Hot Springs Resort
Anaconda, MT 59711
406-797-3241
5, 6

Glacier Mountaineering Touring Center
P.O. Box 261
Emigrant, MT 59072
406-862-5169
1, 2, 3, 4, 5, 6

Hawley Mountain Guest Ranch
P.O. Box 4
McLeod, MT 59052
406-932-2723
1, 3, 5, 6

Izaak Walton Inn
P.O. Box 653
Essex, MT 59916
Phone Essex No. 1
1, 2, 5, 6

Lone Mountain Ranch
P.O. Box 145
Big Sky, MT 59716
406-995-4644
1, 3, 5, 6, 7

Lost Horse Nordic Village
P.O. Box 1553
Hamilton, MT 59840
406-363-9979
1, 2, 3, 4, 5, 6

Yellowstone Nordic
30 Madison Ave.
W. Yellowstone, MT 59758
406-646-7712
1, 2, 3, 4, 5, 6, 7

Nebraska

Camp Moses Merril
P.O. Box 170-a
Linwood, NE 68036
402-666-5639
1, 5, 6, 7

New Hampshire

Attitash Mountain Village
Rte. 302
Bartlett, NH 03812
603-374-2386
1, 2, 5, 6, 7

Balsams/Wilderness
Dixville, NH 03576
603-255-3400
1, 2, 3, 4, 5, 6, 7

Bretton Woods Ski Touring
Rte. 302
Bretton Woods, NH 03575
603-278-5000
1, 2, 3, 4, 5, 6, 7

Charmingfare Inn STC
P.O. Box 128 S. Road
Cnadia, NH 03034
603-483-2307
1, 2, 3, 4, 5, 6, 7

Cold Spring Resort
Ashland, NH 03217
603-536-2214

Darby Field Inn STC
Bald Hill
Conway, NH 03818
603-447-2181
1, 4, 5, 6, 7

Dexter's Inn STC
1 Stage Coach Rd.
Sunapee, NH 03782
603-763-5571

Eastern Slope Inn
Main St.
North Conway, NH 03860
603-356-6321
1, 2, 3, 4, 5, 6, 7

Eastman STC
P.O. Box 53
Grantham, NH 03753
603-863-4444
1, 2, 3, 4, 5, 6, 7

Franconia Inn STC
P.O. Box 116, Easton Rd.
Franconia, NH 03580
603-823-5542
1, 2, 3, 4, 5, 6, 7

Gunstock Ski Area
P.O. Box 336
Laconia, NH 03246
603-293-4341
1, 2, 3, 4, 5, 6, 7

Hollis Hof Ski Touring
53 Richardson Rd.
Hollis, NH 03049
603-465-2633
1, 2, 3, 5, 6, 7

Intervale Nordic Learning Center
Rte. 16A
Intervale, NH 03845
603-356-3379

Jackson Ski Touring Foundation
P.O. Box 216
Jackson, NH 03846
603-383-9355
1, 2, 3, 4, 5, 6, 7

The Ledges Farm
Grantham, NH 03753
603-863-1002
1, 2, 3, 4, 5, 6, 7

Loon Mountain STC
Kancamangus Hwy.
Lincoln, NH 03251
603-745-8111
1, 2, 3, 4, 5, 6, 7

Moose Mountain Lodge
Etna, NH 03750
603-643-3529
1, 2, 3, 5, 6, 7

The Nordic Skier
19 N. Main St.
Wolfboro, NH 03894
603-569-3151
1, 2, 3, 4, 5, 6, 7

Norsk Ski Center
Rte. 11
New London, NH 13257
603-526-4685
1, 2, 3, 4, 5, 6, 7

Pinnacle Mountain STC
Rte. 9
Roxbury, NH 03431
603-363-4703

Road's End Farm
Jackson Hill Rd.
Chesterfield, NH 03443
603-363-4303
1, 2, 3, 5, 6, 7

Sagamore-Hampton
101 N. Rd.
North Hampton, NH 03862
603-964-5341

Snowvillage Ski Touring
Snowville Inn
Snowville, NH 03849
603-447-2818
1, 2, 5, 6, 7

Sugar Hill Inn
Rte. 117
Franconia, NH 03580
603-823-5522
5, 6

Sunset Hill House
Sugar Hill, NH 03585
603-823-5522
1, 2, 3, 4, 5, 6, 7

Temple Mt. Ski Area
Rte. 101
Peterborough, NH 03458
603-924-6949
1, 2, 3, 4, 5, 6, 7

Tory Pines Resort
Francestown, NH 03043
603-588-6352
1, 2, 3, 5, 6

Waterville Estates
P.O. Box 36
Campton, NH 03223
603-726-3082
1, 2, 3, 4, 5, 6, 7

Waterville Valley STC
Waterville Valley, NH 03223
603-236-8311
1, 2, 3, 4, 5, 6, 7

Windblown Ski Touring
New Ipswich, NH 03071
603-878-2869
1, 2, 3, 4, 5, 6, 7

Woodbound Inn
Woodbound Rd.
Jaffery, NH 03452
603-532-8341
1, 2, 3, 4, 5, 6, 7

Ye Olde Allen Farm
1088 Portsmouth Ave.
Greenland, NH 03840
603-436-2861

New Jersey

Craigmeur Ski Area
Newfoundland, NJ 07435
201-697-4501
1, 2, 3, 5, 6, 7

Fairview Lake STC
R.D. 5, P.O. Box 230
Newton, NJ 07860
201-383-9282
1, 2, 3, 5, 6, 7

Great Gorge Ski Area
P.O. Box 848
McAfee, NJ 07428
201-827-2000

The Quarry of Hamburg
Rte. 517N
Hamburg, NJ 07419
201-827-7630
1, 2, 3, 5, 6, 7

Tall Timbers STC
P.O. Box 488
Sussex, NJ 07461
201-875-9904

New Mexico

Angel Fire Nordic Ski Center
P.O. Drawer B
Angel Fire, NM 87710
505-377-2301
1, 2, 3, 4, 5, 6, 7

Miller's XC Ski Tours
P.O. Box 122
Red River, NM 87558

505-754-2374
1, 2, 3, 4, 5, 6, 7

Ski Cloud Country
P.O. Box 287
Cloudcroft, NM 88317
505-682-2333

Taos Ski Valley
Taos, NM 87571
505-776-2291
1, 2, 3, 4, 5, 6, 7

New York

Adirondack Hut to Hut Tours
R.D. 1, P.O. Box 85
Ghent, NY 12075
518-828-7007
2, 3, 5, 6, 7

Adirondack Loj
Lake Placid, NY 12946
518-523-3441
1, 3, 5, 6, 7

Adirondack Ski Tours
Saranac Lake, c/o National Audubon
  Society
950 Third Ave.
New York, NY 10022
212-546-9202
1, 2, 3, 4, 5, 6, 7

Adirondack Wilderness Tours
P.O. Box 52A
Caroga Lake, NY 12032
518-835-4193
1, 2, 3, 5, 6, 7

Adirondack/Woodcroft Ski Touring
  Center
P.O. Box 219
Old Forge, NY 13420
315-369-6031
1, 2, 3, 5, 6, 7

Alpine Recreation Area
298 Ellicot Rd.
Rte. 240
W. Falls, NY 14170
716-662-1400
1, 2, 3, 4, 6, 7

Arrowhead Ski Touring
55 W. Genesee St.
Baldwinsville, NY 13027
315-668-8101
1, 2, 3, 4, 5, 6, 7

Ausable Chasm STC
US 9 and NY 373
Ausable Chasm, NY 12911
518-834-9990
1, 2, 3, 5, 6, 7

The Bark Eater
P.O. Box 139M
Keene, NY 12942
518-576-2221
1, 2, 3, 5, 6, 7

Belleayre Mountain Ski Area
Highmont, NY 12441
914-254-2345
2, 3, 5, 6

The Beresford Farms
R.D. 1

Delanson, NY 12053
518-895-2345
1, 2, 3, 4, 5, 6, 7

Big Tupper Ski Area
P.O. Box 820
Tupper Lake, NY 12986
518-359-3651
1, 2, 4, 5, 6

Big Vanilla Ski Resort
Woodridge, NY 12789
914-434-5321
1, 2, 3, 5, 6

Cascade Ski Touring Center
Rte. 53
Lake Placid, NY 12946
518-523-9605
1, 2, 3, 4, 5, 6, 7

Country Hill STC
North Rd.
Tully, NY 13159
315-357-3041
1, 2, 3, 5, 6, 7

Covewood Lodge
Big Moose Lake
Eagle Bay, NY 13331
315-357-3041
1, 2, 5, 6

Craig Farm Restaurant
Putnam Station, NY 12861
518-547-8336
1, 2, 3, 4, 5, 6, 7

Cunningham's Ski Barn
Gore Mountain
N. Creek, NY 12853
518-251-3215
1, 2, 3, 4, 5, 6, 7

Cunningham's Ski Barn/North Creek
Rte. 28
N. Creek, NY 12853
518-251-3215
1, 2, 3, 4, 5, 6

Drumlins Ski Area
Nottingham Rd.
Syracuse, NY 13201
315-446-3183
1, 2, 3, 4, 5, 6, 7

Erie Bridge Inn
Florence Hill Rd.
R.D. 2
Camden, NY 13316
315-245-1555
1, 2, 3, 5, 6, 7

Four Seasons Ski Center
8012 E. Genesee St.
Fayetteville, NY 13066
315-637-9023
1, 2, 3, 4, 5, 6

Frost Valley YMCA
P.O. Box 97
Olivera, NY 12462
612-985-2291
1, 2, 3, 4, 5, 6, 7

Garnet Hill
13th Lake Rd.

North River, NY 12856
518-251-2821
1, 2, 3, 5, 6, 7

Glens Falls International Cross-Country
   Ski Trails
Glens Falls, NY 12801
518-793-5676
1, 2, 3, 4, 5, 6

Gore Mountain Ski Center
N. Creek, NY 12853
518-251-2411
1, 2, 3, 5, 6

Greek Peak Ski Resort
Cortland, NY 13045
607-835-6111
1, 2, 3, 4, 5, 6, 7

H Bar D Ranch
Norwich, NY 13815
607-334-9752
1, 2, 3, 4, 5, 6, 7

Helderberg Family Campground
Pinnacle Rd.
Voorheesville, NY 12186
518-872-2106
1, 2, 3, 5, 6, 7

Hidden Valley Lake STC
C.P.O. 1190
Kingston, NY 12401
914-338-4616
1, 2, 3, 5, 6, 7

Hyer Meadows X-C
P.O. Box 798
Tannersville, NY 12485
518-589-5361

Inlet Ski Touring Center
Inlet, NY 13360
315-357-6961
1, 2, 3, 4, 5, 6

Inside Edge Ski Touring Center
624 Glen St.
Glens Falls, NY 12801
518-793-5676
1, 2, 3, 4, 5, 6

Lake Minnewaska STC
US 44, NY 55
Lake Minnewaska, NY 12561
914-255-6000

Lake Mohonk Mountain House
New Paltz, NY 12561
914-255-1000
1, 2, 3, 4, 5, 6, 7

Lapland Lake
R.D. 1
Northville, NY 12134
518-863-4974
1, 2, 3, 4, 5, 6, 7

Mt. Van Hoevenberg XC Area
Cascade Rd.
Rte. 73
Lake Placid, NY 12946
518-523-2811
1, 2, 3, 4, 5, 6, 7

Ninety Acres STC
8012 E. Genesee St.
Fayetteville, NY 13066
315-637-9023
1, 2, 3, 4, 5, 6, 7

Old Forge Ski Area
Old Forge, NY 13420
315-369-6983
1, 2, 4, 5, 6, 7

Osceola/Tug Hill XC Ski Center
R.D. 3, P.O. Box 336
Camden, NY 13316
315-599-7377
1, 2, 3, 4, 5, 6, 7

Pechler's Trails
Palmyra, NY 14522
315-597-4210
1, 2, 3, 5, 6, 7

Peek 'n' Peek Recreation
P.O. Box 100
Clymer, NY 14724
716-355-4141
1, 2, 3, 4, 5, 6, 7

Podunk Cross-Country
Podunk Rd.
Trumansburg, NY 14886
607-387-6716
1, 2, 3, 4, 5, 6, 7

The Point
Saranac, NY 12983
518-891-5674
2, 3, 5, 6, 7

Saratoga Spa Ski Touring
Saratoga Springs, NY 12866
518-587-3116

Skaneateles STC at the Sailboat Shop
Rte. 20
Skaneateles, NY 13152
315-685-7558
1, 2, 3, 4, 5, 6, 7

Ski Touring Center at Lake Minnewaska
Lake Minnewaska, NY 12561
914-255-6000
1, 2, 3, 4, 5, 6, 7

Swain Ski Center
Swain, NY 14884
607-545-6511
1, 2, 5, 6

Thunder Mountain Cross-Country Skiing
R.D. 3
Greenwich, NY 12834
1, 2, 3, 5, 6, 7

Twin Pines Touring Center
Rte. 16
Delevan, NY 14042
716-496-5510
2, 3, 4, 5, 6

Ward Pound Ridge Reservation
Cross River, NY 10518
914-763-3493
1, 2, 3, 5, 6, 7

Westport Ski Touring Center
Westport, NY 12993

518-962-8313
1, 2, 4, 5, 6

White Birches Touring Center
Windham, NY 12496
518-734-3266
1, 2, 3, 5, 6, 7

Williams Lake Hotel STC
Williams Lake
Rosendale, NY 12472
212-427-1211
1, 2, 3, 4, 5, 6, 7

North Carolina

Nantahala Outdoor Center
Star Rte.
P.O. Box 68
Bryson City, NC 28713
704-488-2175

Ohio

Dayton X-C Centers
466 Chatham Dr.
Dayton, OH 45429
513-294-0230

Hidden Hollow/Rossignol Touring Center
Opossum Run Rd., Rte. 3
Belleville, OH 44813
419-892-3766
1, 2, 3, 4, 5, 6

North Chagrin Metropark
Rivergrove Winter Sports Area
Willoughby Hills, OH 44094
216-382-7282
1, 2, 3, 5, 6

Ridge Top Golf—STC
701 Pleasant Valley Dr.
Medina, OH 44256
216-725-5520
1, 2, 3, 5, 6, 7

Sleepy Hollow Ski Center
9445 Breckville Rd.
Breckville, OH 44141
216-382-7282
2, 3, 5, 6

Valley View Golf and Ski Club
1212 Cuyahoga
Akron, OH 44313
216-928-9034
1, 2, 3, 4, 5, 6, 7

Oregon

Crater Lake Ski Service
Crater Lake National Park
Crater Lake, OR 97604
503-594-2361
2, 5, 6, 7

Diamond Lake Resort
Diamond Lake, OR 97331
503-793-3333
1, 2, 3, 4, 5, 6, 7

The Inn of the Seventh Mountain
P.O. Box 1207
Bend, OR 97709
503-793-3333
1, 2, 5, 6, 7

Mt. Bachelor Nordic Sports Center
P.O. Box 1031
Bend, OR 97701

503-382-2442
1, 2, 3, 4, 5, 6, 7

Mt. Hood Meadows
P.O. Box 47
Mt. Hood, OR 97041
503-337-2222
1, 2, 3, 4, 5, 6, 7

Odell Lake Lodge
P.O. Box 72
Crescent Lake, OR 97425
503-433-2540

Spout Springs STC
Rte. 1
Weston, OR 97886
503-566-2015

Sunriver Resort
P.O. Box 3212
Sunriver, OR 97702
503-593-1221

Timberline Lodge
Government Camp, OR 97028
503-231-5402
1, 2, 3, 4, 5, 6

Pennsylvania

Apple Valley STC
R.R.D. 1
Zionsville, PA 18092
215-966-5525
1, 2, 3, 4, 5, 6, 7

Crystal Lake Camps
R.D. 1
Hughesville, PA 17737
717-584-2698
1, 2, 3, 4, 5, 6, 7

Denton Hill Ski Area
Rte. 5, Box 367
Coudersport, PA 16915
814-435-2115
1, 4, 5, 6

Hanley's Happy Hill
P.O. Box 67
Eagles Mere, PA 17731
717-525-3461
1, 2, 3, 4, 5, 6, 7

Hidden Valley Farm Inn
R.D. 6, P.O. Box 32
Somerset, PA 15501
814-443-1414
1, 2, 3, 4, 5, 6, 7

Indian Head Nordic Ski Center
Rte. 5, McGahen Hill Rd.
Waterford, PA 16441
814-796-4822
1, 2, 3, 4, 5, 6, 7

The Inn at Starlight Lake
Starlight, PA 18461
717-798-2519
1, 2, 3, 5, 6, 7

Kane Manor Country Inn
230 Clay St.
Kane, PA 16735
814-837-6522
1, 2, 3, 4, 5, 6, 7

Ligonier Mt. Nordic Ski Center
Rte. 30, P.O. Box 206
Laughlintown, PA 15655
412-238-6246

Lindsey Hollow Ski Touring
R.D. 1, P.O. Box 315
Corry, PA 16407
814-664-4461
1, 2, 3, 5, 6, 7

Mountain Streams and Trails Outfitters
P.O. Box 106
Ohiopyle, PA 15470
412-329-8810
1, 2, 3, 4, 5, 6

Nordic Ski Center
Waterford, PA 16441
814-796-4822
1, 2, 3, 4, 5, 6, 7

Seven Springs Mountain Resort
Champion, PA 15622
814-352-7777

Stone Valley Recreation Area
267 Recreation Building
University Park, PA 16802
814-667-3424
1, 2, 3, 4, 5, 6

Starlight Inn
P.O. Box 27
Starlight, PA 18461
717-798-2519

Susquehannock Lodge
Rte. 6, R.D. 1
Ulysses, PA 16948
814-435-2163

Woodland Retreat
P.O. Box 61
Columbus, PA 16405
814-663-1484
1, 2, 3, 5, 6, 7

South Dakota

Pleasant Valley Ski Area
Rte. 1, P.O. Box 256
Gary, SD 57237
605-272-5614
1, 2, 3, 4, 5, 6, 7

Ski Cross-Country
701 Third St.
Spearfish, SD 57983
605-642-3851
1, 2, 3, 4, 5, 6

Utah

Brian Head Cross-Country
P.O. Box 65
Brian Head, UT 84719
801-677-2012
1, 2, 3, 4, 5, 6, 7

Brighton Ski Touring
Brighton Village Store
Brighton, UT 84121
801-649-9156
1, 2, 3, 4, 5, 6, 7

White Pines STC
P.O. Box 680393
Park City, UT 84060
801-649-8701
1, 2, 3, 4, 5, 6, 7

Vermont

Blueberry Hill
Goshen, VT 05477
802-247-6535
1, 2, 3, 4, 5, 6, 7

Blueberry Lake XC Center
c/o L. Robinson
Warren, VT 05674
802-496-6687

BOC Ski Hut
P.O. Box 335
Brattleboro, VT 05301
802-254-8906
1, 2, 3, 4, 5, 6, 7

Bolton Valley Resort
Bolton Valley, VT 05477
802-434-2131
1, 2, 3, 4, 5, 6

Brattleboro Country Club
P.O. Box 335
Brattleboro, VT 05254
802-254-9864
1, 2, 3, 4, 5, 6, 7

Burke Mountain STC
Burke Mountain Recreation, Inc.
E. Burke, VT 05832
802-626-8338
1, 2, 3, 4, 5, 6, 7

Camel's Hump Nordic Ski Center
R.D. 1, P.O. Box 99
Huntington, VT 05462
802-434-2704
1, 2, 3, 4, 5, 6, 7

Catamount Family Center
Fox Run Resort
P.O. Box O
Ludlow, VT 05149
802-879-6001
1, 2, 3, 5, 6, 7

Churchill House Inn and Touring Center
R.D. 3
Brandon, VT 08733
802-247-3300
1, 2, 3, 4, 5, 6, 7

Craftsbury Nordic Center
Craftsbury Common, VT 05827
802-586-2514
1, 2, 3, 4, 5, 6, 7

Darion Ski Touring Center
P.O. Box 101
E. Burke, VT 05832
802-626-5181
1, 2, 3, 4, 5, 6, 7

Edson Hill Ski Touring Center
Stowe, VT 05672
802-253-7371
1, 2, 3, 4, 5, 6, 7

Fox Run Ski Touring Center
R.F.D. 1, P.O. Box 123
Ludlow, VT 05149
802-228-8871
1, 2, 3, 4, 5, 6, 7

Grafton Cross-Country Ski Shop and Trail
Grafton, VT 05363
802-843-2234
1, 2, 3, 4, 5, 6, 7

Green Trails STC
Brookfield, VT 05036
802-276-3412
1, 2, 3, 4, 5, 6, 7

Hermitage Ski Touring
P.O. Box 457
Wilmington, VT 05363
802-464-3759
1, 2, 3, 4, 5, 6

Highland Lodge
P.O. Box 125
Greensboro, VT 05841
802-533-2647
1, 2, 3, 5, 6, 7

Hildene Ski Touring Center
P.O. Box 377
Manchester, VT 05254
802-362-1788
1, 2, 3, 4, 5, 6, 7

Mansfield Touring Center
R.R. 1, Rte. 108
Stowe, VT 05672
802-253-7311
1, 2, 3, 4, 5, 6, 7

Mountain Meadows STC
Killington, VT 05751
802-775-7077
1, 2, 3, 4, 5, 6, 7

Mountain Top STC
P.O. Box 9M
Chittendon, VT 05737
802-483-2311
1, 2, 3, 5, 6, 7

Mt. Ascutney Ski Area
Brownsville, VT 05037
802-484-7711
1, 2, 3, 4, 5, 6, 7

Nordic Inn
Rte. 11, P.O. Box 96
Landgrove, VT 05148
802-824-6444
1, 2, 3, 5, 6, 7

Northern Frontier STC
Montgomery Center, VT 05471
802-229-4044

Ole's Cross-Country
Warren, VT 05673
802-496-3430
1, 2, 3, 4, 5, 6, 7

On the Rocks Lodge
Wilmington, VT 05363
802-464-8364
1, 2, 3, 4, 5, 6, 7

Prospect Mt. Ski Touring
34 West Rd.
Old Bennington, VT 05201
802-442-2575
1, 2, 3, 4, 5, 6, 7

Quechee Inn
P.O. Box 457
Quechee, VT 05059
802-295-3133

Sherman Hollow STC
R.D. 1, P.O. Box 175

Richmond, VT 05477
802-434-2057
1, 2, 3, 4, 5, 6, 7

Sitzmark Ski Touring Center
Mt. Snow Valley
E. Dover Rd.
Wilmington, VT 05363
802-464-8187
1, 2, 3, 4, 5, 6, 7

Ski Tour Vermont
R.F.D. 1, P.O. Box 172
Chester, VT 05143
802-824-6012
1, 2, 3, 5, 6, 7

Snow Valley Ski Touring Center
Londonderry, VT 05148
802-464-8187
1, 2, 3, 4, 5, 6, 7

Stark Farm Ski Touring
Rte. 128
Westford, VT 05494
802-878-2282

Stratton Mountain STC
Stratton Mountain, VT 05155
802-297-2200
1, 2, 3, 4, 5, 6, 7

Sugarbush Inn—Rossignol STC
Rte. 100
Warren, VT 05674
802-583-2301
1, 2, 3, 5, 6, 7

Tater Hill Cross-Country Ski Center
R.F.D. 1
Chester, VT 05143
802-875-2517
1, 2, 3, 4, 5, 6, 7

Topnotch Resort
Mountain Rd., P.O. Box 1260
Stowe, VT 05672
802-253-8585
1, 2, 3, 4, 5, 6, 7

Trapp Family STC
Stowe, VT 05672
802-253-8511
1, 2, 3, 4, 5, 6, 7

Tucker Hill STC
Tucker Hill Lodge
R.D. 1, P.O. Box 146
Waitsfield, VT 05673
802-496-3983
1, 2, 3, 4, 5, 6, 7

Viking Ski Touring Center
Little Pond Rd.
Londonderry, VT 05148
802-824-3933
1, 2, 3, 4, 5, 6, 7

The White House
P.O. Box 757
Wilmington, VT 05363
802-464-2135
1, 2, 3, 4, 5, 6, 7

Wilderness Trails Nordic Ski School
Marshland Farm
Quechee, VT 05059

802-295-7620
1, 2, 3, 4, 5, 6, 7

Wild Wings STC
P.O. Box 132
Peru, VT 05152
803-824-6973
1, 2, 3, 4, 5, 6, 7

Woodstock Ski Touring Center
Woodstock, VT 05091
802-824-6793
1, 2, 3, 4, 5, 6, 7

Washington

The Cross-Country Center
P.O. Box 118
Snoqualmie, WA 98068
509-434-6646

49 Degree N.
P.O. Box 166
Chewelah, WA 99109
509-935-6649
1, 2, 3, 4, 5, 6

Mountainholm Touring Center
P.O. Box 37
Easton, WA 98925
206-623-7318
1, 2, 3, 5, 6, 7

Scottish Lake Cross-Country Ski Area
P.O. Box 312
Leavenworth, WA 98826
509-548-7330
1, 2, 3, 5, 6

Sun Mountain Lodge
P.O. Box 1000
Winthrop, WA 98862
509-996-2211
1, 2, 3, 4, 5, 6, 7

West Virginia

Snowshoe Ski Area
Snowshoe, WV 26209
304-572-4636

Whitegrass Ski Touring
Rte. 1, P.O. Box 37
Davis, WV 26260
304-866-4114
1, 2, 3, 5, 6, 7

Wisconsin

Afterglow Trail
2565 Nicolet Forest Rd.
Phelps, WI 54554
715-545-2560

Blackhawk Ridge
P.O. Box 92
Sauk, WI 53583
608-643-3775
1, 2, 3, 4, 5, 6, 7

Brigham Farm Cross-Country Skiing
Blue Mounds, WI 53517
608-437-3038
1, 2, 3, 5, 6, 7

Camp 10
Rte. 17, County A
Rhinelander, WI 53005
715-362-6754

Castle Rock Country Club
Rte. 2, P.O. Box 181E
New Lisbon, WI 53950
608-847-7200

Chanticleer Inn
1458 E. Bollar Lake Rd.
Eagle River, WI 54521
715-479-4486
1, 2, 3, 5, 6

Devil's Head Lodge
P.O. Box 38
Merrimac, WI 53561
608-493-2251
1, 5, 6

Devil's Lake State Park
Rte. 4
Baraboo, WI 53913
608-356-6618

Eagle River Nordic Center
P.O. Box 936
Eagle River, WI 54421
715-479-7285
1, 2, 3, 4, 5, 6, 7

Game Unlimited Cross-Country Ski Area
Rte. 2, P.O. Box 351
Hudson, WI 54016
715-246-5475
1, 2, 5, 6, 7

Gateway Lodge
P.O. Box 147
Land O' Lakes, WI 54540
715-547-3321

Green Lake Ski Trails
Green Lake, WI 53965
414-294-3323
1, 2, 3, 4, 5, 6, 7

Haven North Trails
Lake Michele
Hurley, WI 54534
715-561-5626

Heritage Ridge Trails
Hwy. 83
Delafield, WI 53018
414-646-8405

Hoofbeat Ridge Ranch
Mazomanie, WI 53560
608-767-2593
1, 2, 3, 4, 5, 6, 7

Iola Winter Sports Club
P.O. Box 234
Waupaca, WI 54981
715-445-3411

Johnson Park Nordic
Racine Parks and Recreation
Racine, WI 53403
414-636-9229

Lake Owen Lodge
Lake Owen
Cable, WI 54821
715-798-3785

Minocqua Winter Park
Nordic Ski Center
P.O. Box 558

Minocqua, WI 54548
715-356-3309
1, 2, 3, 4, 5, 6, 7

Mt. Hardscrabble Ski Area
Rice Lake, WI 54868
715-234-3412
1, 2, 3, 4, 5, 6, 7

Mt. LaCrosse
P.O. Box 9
LaCrosse, WI 54602
608-788-0044
1, 2, 3, 4, 5, 6, 7

Olympia Resort and Spa
Oconomowoc, WI 53066
414-567-0311
1, 2, 5, 6

Palmquist's Farm
River Rd.
Brantwood, WI 54513
715-564-2558
1, 2, 3, 4, 5, 6, 7

Sky Line Ski Area
Rte. 3
Friendship, WI 53934
608-339-3421
1, 2, 3, 5, 6

Steed's Wolf River Lodge
White Lake, WI 54491
715-882-2182
1, 2, 3, 4, 5, 6

Telemark Lodge
Cable, WI 54821
715-798-3811
1, 2, 3, 4, 5, 6, 7

Trees for Tomorrow Center
Eagle River, WI 54521
715-479-6456
1, 2, 3, 4, 5, 6

Trollhaugen
P.O. Box 607
Dresser, WI 54009
715-755-2950

Wild Wolf Inn
Hwy. 44
White Lake, WI 54491
715-882-8611

Wintergreen Ski Touring Center
P.O. Box 467
Spring Green, WI 53588
608-588-2571

Winter Sports Center
Green Lake, WI 54941
414-294-3271
1, 2, 3, 6, 7

Woodside Ranch Resort
Rte. 3
Mauston, WI 53948
608-847-4275
1, 2, 3, 4, 5, 6, 7

Wyoming

Cross-Country Connection
1774 Jackson
Laramie, WY 82070
307-721-2851
1, 2, 3, 4, 5, 6, 7

Darwin Ranch Nordic Ski Lodge and
    Guide Service
P.O. Box 511
Jackson, WY 83001
208-354-2767
1, 4, 5, 6, 7

Flagg Ranch
P.O. Box 187
Moran, WY 83013
800-443-2311
1, 2, 5, 6

Grand Targee
Alta, WY
(via Driggs, ID 83422)
307-353-2304
1, 2, 3, 4, 5, 6

Jackson Hole Cross-Country
P.O. Box 290
Teton Village, WY 83025
800-443-2311
1, 2, 3, 4, 5, 6, 7

Jackson Hole Nordic Ski Center
P.O. Box 1226
Jackson, WY 83001
307-733-2026
1, 2, 3, 4, 5, 6, 7

Togwotee Mountain Lodge
P.O. Box 91
Moran, WY 83013
307-543-2847
1, 2, 3, 4, 5, 6, 7

TWA Services, Inc.
Yellowstone National Park, WY 82190
800-421-3401
1, 2, 5, 6

University of Wilderness
P.O. Box 410
Centennial, WY 82055
307-721-3867
1, 2, 3, 5, 6

Wind River Ranch
P.O. Box 278
Dubois, WY 82513
307-721-3867
1, 2, 3, 4, 5, 6

Selected Bibliography

For more in-depth or advanced information on technique, racing, warm-ups, diet, and history of the sport, I recommend browsing through any of the following.

Anderson, Robert, *The Complete Book of Stretching* (Bolinas, Calif.: Shelter Publications, 1980)

Every active person should have a copy of *The Complete Book of Stretching* close at hand. Even armchair athletes will find important information.

The book contains stretches for everything from raquetball to aerobic dancing. Included are complete diagrams and descriptions of each of the stretches. Mr. Anderson has helpful hints on warming up, proper nutrition, and care for your back. I found the back exercises particularly helpful.

Arnot, Robert Burns, and Charles Latham Gaines, *SportSelection* (New York: Viking Press, 1984)

Selecting the best sport for your own particular needs is done in many cases by trial and error. I found the sport to fit my temperament only after engaging in a number of other sports that were not as fulfilling as cross-country skiing. If I had been able to use a book such as *SportSelection* in the early going, it might not have been so hard to arrive at what now seems like an inevitable conclusion.

However, the tests outlined in *SportSelection* need not be the final word in choosing a sport (I could not do the Blind Stork test for the life of me), but rather a starting point for those who want to pursue a single sport more actively, or are just interested in the physical requirements of the various sports described in the book.

In addition, the book is a readable primer on physiology and the other control systems of sports. I recommend it for more in-depth reading.

Barnett, Steve, *Cross-Country Downhill and other Nordic Mountain Techniques* (Seattle, Wash.: Pacific Search Press, 1979)

The premier telemark skier in the United States before the notion of skiing downhill on cross-country skis was popular, Steve Barnett offers a look at another way to ski downhill. He was one of the first converts from Alpine to test cross-country skis in downhill and steep outback areas of our national forests. Much of the equipment he first used would be termed totally unsuitable by today's standards.

I like telemarking because it requires more finesse to negotiate the slopes on cross-country skis than rigid plastic boots and short, fast-turning Alpine skis require. Alpine equipment compensates for many errors.

The book may seem out of date, but it comes strongly recommended if you're hoping to attempt to learn the telemarking technique; the precepts still are quite good. The technique is wonderful and well worth exploring, as it adds to your skiing repertoire and enjoyment.

Beinhorn, George (ed.), *Food for Fitness* (New York: Anderson World, 1975) A solid guide to nutrition for the athlete.

Bergh, Ulf, *The Physiology of Cross-Country Ski Racing* (Champaign, Ill.: Human Kinetics Publishers, 1982)

Ulf Bergh must have taken apart the telephone when he was six years old to see exactly how it functioned. *The Physiology of Cross-Country Ski Racing* was written for those who have an insatiable curiosity to find out the inner workings of the skier's body. In the Scandinavian countries they take their cross-country skiing seriously; consequently they have physiological information about it available comparable to what Americans know about pitcher's elbow and football knees.

Michael Brady and Marianne Hadler have translated from the Swedish this excellent description of what goes on in your body during racing and training for cross-country skiing. The book describes in depth physical performance factors, cell function during exercise, oxygen uptake and what it means, as well as other tidbits. The book is the perfect companion for a better understanding of Marty Hall's and John Caldwell's chapters on physiology. Bergh condenses an enormous amount of information about a complicated facet of skiing.

Brody, Jane, *Jane Brody's Nutrition Book,* (New York: W. W. Norton, 1981)

Caldwell, John, *Caldwell on Cross-Country: Training and Technique for the Serious Skier* (Brattleboro, Vt.: Stephen Greene Press, 1975)

   This advanced version of Caldwell's previous book, *The Cross-Country Ski Book*, might be called the graduate course of study in cross-country skiing. *Caldwell on Cross-Country* details the refinements and perfections of his coaching philosophy, now called the "Putney Method."

   Although the racing scene has been radicalized with the advent of the skating technique, the fundamentals of racing and training remain the same. The book is a classic and probably will remain so, in much the same way that Izaak Walton has remained the "Compleat Angler."

Fehr, Lucy M., *Cross-Country Skiing: A Guide to America's Best Trails* (New York: William Morrow & Company, 1979)

   If you feel confident enough to ski off the beaten path, this book will tell you where to go. Fehr has listed in great detail some of the best trails in the United States. In addition to the touring centers, she has listed some of the finest wilderness touring in this country.

   Winter is as unpredictable as a horse race, so it is always advisable to call ahead to check on skiing conditions and to make sure a particular entry isn't out of date. It can be disheartening to arrive and find higher prices, a haven for snowmobiles, or a "Closed Until Further Notice" sign. One bad winter can ruin a touring center.

Gaskill, Steven, *A Basic Guide to Competitive Cross-Country Skiing, Part One and Part Two* (Park City, Utah: USST, 84060)

   In-depth writing on competitive cross-country skiing training by the United States Ski Team staff. Included are notes on off- and in-season training, ski selection, making hairies, and much more. These two volumes outline the philosophy behind much of the work now going on at the international levels with the United States Cross-Country Ski Team.

Gillette, Ned, *Cross-Country Skiing* (Seattle, Wash.: The Mountaineers, 1979)

   An excellent book by the premier adventure skier in the United States, Ned Gillette. Ned has brought his many years of experience to the pages of *Cross-Country Skiing*—experiences gained from journeys throughout the Canadian Arctic hauling sleds, skiing around Mount Everest, and skiing the roof of New Zealand. His subtle Vermont wit is evident on every page, and with the help of John Dostal he has produced a highly readable book.

   Gillette's chapters on technique are especially enlightening. He brings alive a potentially dull subject and paints a clear picture of how to ski efficiently and easily. His chapters on wilderness touring and winter survival focus on little-discussed sides of the sport.

Haas, Robert, *Eat to Win: The Sports Nutrition Bible* (New York: Rawson Associates, 1984)

This book covers every aspect of nutrition for the serious athlete. Robert Haas has developed nutrition programs for Martina Navratilova and other premier athletes.

Hall, Marty, with Pam Penfold, *One Stride Ahead: An Expert's Guide to Cross-Country Skiing* (Tulsa, Okla.: Winchester Press, 1981)

If *Caldwell on Cross-Country* has been called the "Bible of the Sport," then it is fair to call *One Stride Ahead* its New Testament. Marty Hall has consolidated his expertise gained from twenty years of working with both American and Canadian cross-country ski teams and compiled it into a book. Five years have not diminished the import of this book. It is still useful for the person who wants to take the sport of cross-country skiing seriously. A revised edition is in the making.

The book covers in fine detail every aspect of racing, whether you are preparing for your first marathon race or heading to the Olympic trails. If you become serious about the local citizens' racing circuit, the Great American Ski Chase, or national competitions, Hall's book will keep you at least one stride ahead.

Kraus, Barbara, *Calories & Carbohydrates, Fifth Edition Revised* (New York: NAL, 1984)

Woodward, Bob, *Cross-Country Ski Conditioning: For Exercise Skiers and Citizen Racers* (Chicago: Contemporary Books, 1983)

If you are planning to take up serious cross-country ski racing, or just trying to adapt cross-country skiing to your work schedule, Bob Woodward's book is a must. It's the perfect book for nine-to-fivers. As I read this book through, I felt it was a good companion to the *Cross-Country Skier's Handbook*.

After you have read the *Cross-Country Skier's Handbook* through and have skied a winter or two, you may want to start racing. The ski-related conditioning program in *Cross-Country Ski Conditioning* provides the information in clear and concise terms to prepare you for your more rigorous commitment. The book will provide guidance and help you get more out of your training.

The following periodicals report on cross-country skiing.

Cross-Country Skier
P.O. Box 1203
Brattleboro, VT 05301
802-257-1304
This magazine is dedicated to cross-country skiing and comes out five times a year.

Nordic West
P.O. Box 7077
Bend, OR 97708
Three-times-a-year informative and exciting Nordic skiing articles.

Outside
Mariah Publications Corporations
P.O. Box 2690
Boulder, CO 80321
Occasional articles on cross-country skiing, terrific photos, and writing on other outdoor subjects.

Ski
380 Madison Ave.
New York, NY 10017
212-687-3000
Mostly aimed at Alpine skiers but has occasional articles on cross-country skiing.

Skiing
One Park Ave.
New York, NY 10016
212-725-3800
Directed at the Alpine consumer, with occasional articles on cross-country skiing.

Ski Racing
P.O. Box 70
Fair Haven, VT 05743
802-468-5666
A weekly newspaper dedicated to skiing, with an occasional section, called "SR Nordic," dedicated to Nordic skiing. The best way to keep up with the team in Europe.

Ultra Sport
11 Beacon St.
Boston, MA 02108
617-227-1988
A magazine for the ultimate long-distance junkie. Good in-depth articles on people involved in sports such as cross-country skiing. Even an occasional article on a cross-country skier.

Index
